Bible Study *for* Joy *and* Profit

a practical, nondenominational guide
to mining Scriptural treasures…

Charlie Brackett

Clarion Word Publishing
clarionword.com

Bible Study for Joy and Profit

Copyright © 2006, 2007, 2008 by Charlie Brackett

 Published by Clarion Word Publishing
www.clarionword.com

Second Edition

Second Printing

Most Scripture taken from the New King James Version.
Copyright © 1982 by Thomas Nelson, Inc. Used by permission.
All rights reserved.

KJV Scripture taken from The King James Version.

NIV® Scripture taken from the Holy Bible, New International Version®.
Copyright © 1973, 1978, 1984 International Bible Society.
Used by permission of Zondervan. All rights reserved.

NASV® Scripture taken from the New American Standard Bible®,
Copyright © 1960,1962,1963,1968,1971,1972,1973,1975,1977, 1995
by The Lockman Foundation. Used by permission.

Clarion Word Publishing
P. O. Box 21277
Chattanooga, TN 37424, USA
www.clarionword.com

ISBN 9781934821046

This book is dedicated with gratitude to
all faithful Bible teachers who realize that
teaching is more than simply imparting
knowledge and who understand theirs is the
noble work of changing behavior...

and to all Bible students who are cultivating
a love for God's truth.

Table of Contents

Preface

This book is about how to study. As much as how, it is about why. How to study and why we should seem to this writer immensely important for each of us, but are topics in which many of us have never been formally trained. I went through secondary and high school without much effort and always seemed to make good grades. I graduated high in my class, but then came university. Somehow things were tougher. Much about which I was graded came by way of a lecturing professor who seemed unconcerned about my learning, or even if I was in my seat. It was a different world. I had made good grades in reading, writing and arithmetic, even history and calculus, but here was a world of much greater knowledge, and I had no clue how to unlock it. No one had ever taught me how to study. Not only was it not a subject for formal study at the high school level, it was not available as a course at the university. My grades and my interest in learning plummeted.

It was not until I was thrown into the business world that I learned how to study. It was necessary for survival. Ambition instilled by my father drove me to get ahead, and each step required new knowledge and new skills. As my own family began to grow and mature, I became more interested and involved in the work of the church. Wherever I turned and whatever task I laid hand to required learning. Anyone who attends the services of the church does not attend long before hearing someone emphasize how much we all need to study God's Word. Preachers, elders and Bible teachers are always saying it, and they should. The question is how many members of the Lord's church are personally studying? Or maybe the more pertinent question is how many know how to effectively study for themselves?

Countless times I have wished that I had been required, even forced, early on to take a course in how and why to study. To whatever degree there is still the gap I experienced in the formal education of our young or a lack of study skills in members of the Lord's church, it is hoped that this book will help fill that need.

This book is about more than how to study. From beginning to end an effort has been made to convince the reader that there is joy in study – not just in the joy of having a saving relationship with God, but in the joy available in the process of study: the joy of discovery, the joy of achieving, the joy of knowing, and the subsequent joy available in teaching others. Since joy is possible only for those who finish their study, a number of pages are devoted to how to motivate oneself in personal study.

After each chapter, there are questions designed to help you review the material covered. They are suitable and profitable for group discussion making this an ideal textbook for classes in home or church.

Throughout, there has been an attempt to deal with Biblical matters without denominational bias. Though some positions taken may be controversial, they are not included for the sake of controversy. A nondenominational approach will, no doubt, offend some. While that is regrettable, agreement with any denominational view is necessarily divisive. Truth is unified and consistent. God's Word is truth and does not sanction nor promote denominational division. Is my exegesis of every Biblical passage correct? Maybe not. I realize my own fallibility, but in the firm belief that everyone can understand God's Word for him or herself, I am striving to know the truth more perfectly without the influence or approval of theologians and human creeds. I challenge you to do the same. If you find I have misunderstood or misapplied the truth, you would be my friend to show me the way more perfectly.

May the Lord help you cultivate a deep, abiding love of truth and discover the unique joy of unlocking the treasures of His Word for yourself. There is joy in both the unlocking and the treasures to be uncovered, and no one of us is very far from embracing that joy.

Charlie Brackett
charlie@clarionword.com

"You shall know the truth, and the truth shall make you free."

The Book We All Need to Study

Is the Bible really God's Word?

But what if today's Bible is not what was written?

It is appropriate as we start learning how to study to consider the nature of the book we have chosen as the focus of our study. Many books are worthy of study. If you want to become a civil engineer, it will be not only helpful but necessary to study several texts recognized as authoritative in the field. A geologist will want to consider what those who have gone before have learned. He or she will need to wrestle with the chemistry of rocks and the physical effects of the elements on geological formations. Study, study, study. And at the heart of the activity is always the information – whether contained in a traditional book or on the Worldwide Web – which unlocks the course of our career, helps us achieve a goal, or in some other way enriches life.

It is this book's thesis that there is one book superior to all the rest. One book whose message is more valuable for this life and whatever follows than any other book, more authoritative

1

than the highest edicts and governments of men. That book is the Bible, the Holy Word of God.

What Is The Bible?

In many ways, the Bible is a unique book. It is actually a collection of sixty-six books, and yet is so integrated it can be realistically called one book. It was written by approximately forty men, very different in their educational levels, stations in society, outlooks on life, cultures and periods of history in which they lived. What they wrote is so singular in its message and consistent in its presentation it can properly be called one book.

The last of it was written almost 2,000 years ago. Since then, since even hundreds of years before the New Testament writings, countless men and women have devoted their lives to protecting, copying and analyzing it. Dozens of translations have been published, and though the work of fallible men, their accuracy can be comparatively evaluated and attested. We can be assured that the essential message we have today is faithful to what was written thousands of years ago. Those who have protected and reproduced it did their work in the face of many antagonists bent on maligning God's Word. In every century, its enemies have tried to destroy it. Yet it remains unchanged and untarnished, and every year the Bible continues to be the best selling book of all time.

We can be certain that when we study it we have God's message as it was originally given. While unique among books, it is to be studied like all other books. It presents characters, describes scenes, relates history, presents profound truths of life, and challenges the very depths of man's behavior and knowledge in virtually every realm of fundamental human study. It was written for and is easily understood by the common man and woman, yet challenges the intellectual. It is possible for anyone who wants to know it to know it well.

The principles, attitudes and skills we will discuss throughout the following chapters will help you in your journey to greater understanding of the Bible, the book that claims to be the very words of God Almighty. The things we will discuss are practical and down-to-earth. They will not only help you understand the Bible better, many will help you more effectively study any book, learn anything more completely.

What Does The Bible Claim For Itself?

If we summed up all of the divine claims the Bible makes for itself, we would be forced to conclude that there is no book under heaven more worthy of our study time, our complete attention, our careful analysis, and our diligent application to life. We will notice a few of its claims.

It claims to be the Word of God

The apostle Paul taught that all Scripture is given by the inspiration of God – according to the Greek, "God *breathed*" (2 Timothy 3:16) – and that what he and other inspired writers wrote was revealed to them not by men but by the Holy Spirit who had searched the deep things of God and given them those things of God's mind that He wanted mankind to know (1 Corinthians 2:10-13).

It claims to be the absolute truth

David referred to God's law as truth (Psalm 119:142), and in another place he pleaded that God's Word of truth not be taken from his mouth (Psalm 119:43). Some are prone to question as did Pilate, "What is truth?" (John 18:38) They may argue that each one has his own truth, in fact, is entitled to his own. In its claim to be God's Word, the Bible stands opposed to that view. It presents the truth as a way of understanding and living above the wisdom of men for it insists that "There is a way that seems right to a man, But its end is the way of death." (Proverbs 14:12)

Jesus prayed regarding His disciples, "Sanctify them by Your truth, Your word is truth." (John 17:17) Further, the Bible calls Jesus the Word (John 1:1), and reports that He said of Himself, "I am the way, *the truth* and the life." (John 14:6)

It claims purity

In fact, the Bible claims that every single Word of God is pure (Proverbs 30:5), and goes on to say that if anyone adds to His Word, thus tampering with its purity, He will rebuke that one, and he will be found a liar (Proverbs 30:6). The poet David said, "The law of the Lord is perfect…" (Psalm 19:7) It is without blemish or any form of imperfection. It is incorruptible (1 Peter 1:23). We are to desire the pure milk of God's Word that by it we may grow (1 Peter 2:2). Not only will we grow by learning and living its teachings, our souls will be purified and made fit for eternity with the Author of all purity (1 Peter 1:22).

It claims completeness

When the apostle Paul wrote to the young man Timothy, he described Scripture as being inspired of God – all of it (2 Timothy 3:16). The mere idea of it coming to us by God's instigation suggests its completeness. Can you think of Almighty God, the Creator of the universe, creating anything that was left unfinished or incomplete? Still, Paul went on as if to make certain that Timothy and we make no mistake about God's Word. He said that Scripture was given "that the man of God may be complete, thoroughly equipped for every good work." (2 Timothy 3:17) Do we need anything else? No! Why? God's Word, the Bible, is complete for guiding us in all good work.

It claims to be the only means of faith in God

Faith is the only reality we have today for something we hope for in the future (Hebrews 11:1). What we believe about anything (our conviction) is based upon evidence. We consider what evidence is available and either believe or not depending on how strong and convincing we perceive the evidence to be. For example, suppose you believe you will go on a cruise in the Mediterranean with your friend next year. Why do you believe that? Perhaps for several reasons: your friend has agreed that a cruise with you would be nice and that next year is a good time. Cruise ships are sailing now and there is no reason to believe that all of the cruise lines will shut down by next year. You are both healthy. You believe you will have the necessary fare in time to book your cabin. The United States is not at war with any country around the Mediterranean Sea. And there are more reasons. Suppose, however, before next year a war breaks out in the region, or one of you comes down with a debilitating disease, or someone steals your financial nest egg. The hope you have for the cruise suddenly goes out the window because the evidence which supported your belief is seriously damaged.

"Faith is the substance of things hope for, the evidence of things not seen." (Hebrews 11:1) Faith is not blind. What we believe about God the Father, about the Bible and about Jesus Christ is all based on evidence. That is one reason it is important that you study the Bible. Bible study is all about acquiring and analyzing faith-building evidence, because faith comes by hearing the Word of God (Romans 10:17).

It claims to be able to save us

Jesus said, "And you shall know the truth, and the truth shall make you free." (John 8:32) Free from what? Why, free from ignorance, of course. But much, much more than that – free from sin and death. Jesus also said, "...he who hears My word and believes in Him who sent Me has everlasting life, and shall not come into judgment, but has passed from death into life." (John 5:24) Paul wrote to the Roman church proclaiming the gospel as God's power to save, not only to the Jew, but also to all men (Romans 1:16). I like the way the apostle Peter styled this power of God's Word when he said, "…you have purified your souls in obeying the truth…" (1 Peter 1:22)

It claims to be eternal

"The grass withers, the flower fades, But the word of our God stands forever." (Isaiah 40:8) Peter quoted this thought from Isaiah when he spoke of the everlasting Word of God in his first letter (1 Peter 1:22-25). He likened God's Word, the Bible, to incorruptible seed, "…which lives and abides forever." (1 Peter 1:23) And Jesus Himself announced, "Heaven and earth will pass away, but My words will by no means pass away." (Mark 13:31)

It claims to be that which will judge us

There is an interesting description of the Word of God in the Hebrew letter. There we find that God's Word is "living and powerful, and sharper than any two-edged sword, piercing even to the division of the soul and spirit, and of joints and marrow, and is a discerner of the thoughts and intents of the heart." (Hebrews 4:12) Is this speaking of the words on the pages of a book, or is it speaking of Jesus Christ? After all, Jesus did say He is the truth (John 14:6), and the gospel of John speaks of the Word being in the beginning with God, that Word being God (John 1:1) and becoming flesh and dwelling among men (John 1:14). Whatever the Hebrews writer had in mind, make no mistake, God's Word is living and powerful and able to discern our innermost thoughts and intents. It is capable of judging us, but will it? Jesus answered in the affirmative when He said, "He who rejects Me, and does not receive My words, has that which judges him – the word that I have spoken will judge him in the last day." (John 12:48)

Any one of these claims the Bible makes for itself should be sufficient to make us want to study it.

Are the Bible's Claims Believable?

Many today ask if, through all the copies and ages separating us from the original writers, the accuracy of the Bible, particularly the New Testament, was preserved. It is a good question.

It is logical that the same God who wrote the Bible also preserved it. Can there be any doubt that the intelligence, wisdom and power which produced the Bible are able also to safeguard it from change or destruction and deliver it intact to succeeding generations. God not only could, but he wanted to keep His Word intact for the same reasons He wanted to communicate to man in the first place. Allowing His message to be destroyed or tampered with in any way would defeat God's purpose for the creation of man and, therefore, the universe. Given what the Bible says about who God is – His power and His wisdom – this possibility is not only illogical, it is unthinkable.

God is Obligated to Protect His Word

God's claims about His Word necessitated that He protect it until now. The Bible claims it will endure forever thus implying endurance in original form. By claiming His Word will last forever (Mark 13:31; 1 Pet. 1:23, 25), God would have to take whatever steps needed to assure that no one destroys it.

By claiming His Word is perfect God obligated Himself to protect it from tampering (Proverbs 30:5; James 1:25; 1 Peter 2:2; Deuteronomy 4:2; 12:32; Revelation 22:18, 19).

By claiming His Word is all-sufficient, God obligated Himself to preserve it to do the work for which He claimed nothing else was needed (2 Timothy 3:17; Jude 3).

Evaluating the accuracy of what we have today involves two questions: 1) how reliable are the sources from which our Bibles were translated?, and 2) how accurately did the translators do their job? This latter question is dealt with more thoroughly in Chapter 6 in the discussion about using various translations. Suffice to say here, translations are the work of uninspired, fallible men, and as such, have errors in them. As it turns out, errors in translations by scholarly committees are slight and do not materially affect the message as God gave it to mankind. (More on this in Chapter 12 under *Inerrancy of Scripture*.)

Secular records indicate that God is, in fact, preserving His Word. Despite attempts throughout history to eliminate the Bible and its influence, the Bible continues to have its impact on the world today. Since original documents are not available to us now, how reliable are the copies we have? There is a tremendous amount of evidence substantiating reliability of our Bible versions, enough to fill volumes. This is not the place for a lengthy presentation of such evidence, but a few thoughts are in order.

Biblical Text Passes Reliability Tests

There are three basic principles used in the field of historiography for testing historical reliability of ancient writings:

(1) The bibliographical test

(2) The internal test

(3) The external test

The Bibliographical Test

The bibliographical test alone shows the Bible message to have been transmitted through manuscript copies to our time with no consequential change. Other ancient documents, compared to the Bible, have surprisingly little evidence to support the authenticity of the copies now in our possession, yet we accept them without question. Based on current evidence, no other ancient literature is nearly as trustworthy as the Bible. While there are several points of comparison that prove this statement, one should be sufficient for our purpose.

In his *Chapters in the History of New Testament Textual Criticism,* Bruce Metzger makes this observation: "Of all the literary compositions by the Greek people, the Homeric poems are the best suited for comparison with the Bible... In the entire range of ancient Greek and Latin literature, the *Iliad* ranks next to the New Testament in possessing the greatest amount of manuscript testimony."[1] The original writings for both of these documents have been lost, so we work from the most ancient copies available. Whether or not our copies of the Iliad are accurate is generally not questioned, though many claim that our copies of the New Testament are corrupted. Comparing the two shows substantial reason to believe that the New Testament is more reliable:[2]

Works	Written	Earliest Copy	Time Span	No. of Copies
Iliad	900 B.C.	400 B.C.	500 years	643
New Testament	40-100 A.D.	125 A.D.	25 years	over 24,000

The bibliographical test clearly demonstrates reasons to believe that copies of the New Testament are the most credible of ancient documents.

The Internal Test

There are three types of internal evidences that the Bible is God's Word and can be trusted. The first is its unique unity. As noted earlier, there are sixty-six books written by forty men over a span

1 McDowell, Josh, *Evidence That Demands a Verdict, Volume 1,* (1990), p. 43, Here's Life Publishers, San Bernadino, CA, citing Metzger, Bruce, *Chapters in the History of New Testament Textual Criticism,* p. 144, Grand Rapids: William B. Eerdmans Publishing Co., 1963.
2 Ibid.

of 1,500 years, and though it covers hundreds of controversial subjects, the authors all spoke with agreement. There are no contradictions. From beginning to end, there is one message – God's redemption of mankind.

The second internal evidence is fulfilled prophecy. The Bible contains hundreds of detailed prophecies relating to the future of individual nations, certain cities, the whole of mankind, to certain people and to the coming of one who would be the Savior of not only Israel, but all who would believe in Him. Unlike prophecies in other religious books, Biblical prophecies are extremely detailed and have neither failed to come to pass or to be accurate in all of their details. There are over three hundred prophecies of Jesus Christ alone, each one accurately and completely fulfilled. (See more about the power of fulfilled prophecy in Chapter 4.) Fulfilled prophecies in the Bible attest not only to the authenticity of Scripture but to its divine origin. The Bible simply had to come from God.

The unique authority and power of the Bible message is another area of internal evidence. Countless lives have been changed by its instruction. Whether it speaks of correct behavior, healthy living, good management, effective teaching, salesmanship, communication, positive thinking, conflict resolution, marriage, or child rearing, its words are authoritative and its counsel is wise. No good advice found in today's books on these subjects is in conflict with Biblical principles penned long ago before men had discovered for themselves the matters in human psychology and relationships now considered wholesome and workable.

All internal evidence supports the conviction that the Bibles we hold in our hands are from God and can be trusted.

The External Test

The external test seeks to find other historical material outside the Bible that will confirm or deny its accuracy, reliability and authenticity. One such source is the body of other early documents. The list of early writers that considered the Bible accurate is long: Eusebius, Papias, Irenaeus, Ignatius, Clement of Rome, Polycarp, the Jewish historian Flavius Josephus, and others. The Biblical quotes of these and other writers are so complete they can be used to precisely reconstruct the text of the Bible as we have it today.

Another source of external confirmation is archaeology. Merrill Unger notes, "Old Testament archaeology has rediscovered whole nations, resurrected important peoples, and in a most astonishing manner filled in historical gaps, adding immeasurably to the knowledge of Biblical backgrounds."[3] Consideration of all available supporting archaeological evidence deserves its own volume of books. Before leaving the subject to other books, let's notice a couple of quotes about the Bible from noted archaeologists:

> Archaeologist Joseph Free said, "Archaeology has confirmed countless passages which had been rejected by critics as unhistorical or contrary to known facts."[4]

> Renowned Jewish archaeologist Nelson Gluek made this startling statement: "It... may be stated categorically that no archaeological discovery has ever controverted a Biblical reference. Scores of archeological findings have been made which confirm in clear outline or exact detail historical statements in the Bible."[5]

Having considered all of the evidence (bibliographical, internal and external), Josh McDowell stated, "The logical conclusion based upon evidence is that if one rejects the Bible as being reliable, then, if he is consistent and uses the same tests, he must

3 Ibid, citing Unger, Merrill F., *Archaeology and the Old Testament*, Rev. ed., p. 15, Chicago: Moody Press, 1954. Used by permission.
4 Free, Joseph, *Archaeology and Bible History*, (1969), p. 1, Scripture Press, Wheaton, Illinois.
5 Glueck, Nelson, *Rivers in the Desert*, (1959), p. 136, Farar, Straus and Cudahy, New York.

The External Test

throw out all classical literature and disregard their historical testimony."[6]

How Difficult Is the Bible to Understand?

It is not uncommon to hear someone say they do not study the
Bible because it is too difficult to understand. While some may
not be willing to admit this reason for not studying, they rarely
or never attempt to pursue a Bible question or try to grasp a
spiritual concept on their own. They get their learning from a
preacher or competent Bible teacher. Sadly, many adult teachers
and some elders of the church are not able to dig out the meat
of God's Word for themselves, but rely on a class book to lay out
the points and the passages for them. Is that because the Bible is
just too difficult? Certainly not!

Are there difficult passages in the Bible? Yes, of course. Still, your
Bible on the whole is not a difficult book. It may surprise you to
know that the most commonly used English translations are written at the reading level of a twelfth grade student or younger. The
King James Version reading level is at the 12th grade level , the
New American Standard at the 11th, the New King James at 8.5,
the Living Bible at 8.3, and the New International Version at 7.8.[7]
A new (first published in 2001) translation, the English Standard Version – arguably the most literal of English translations – is reported by
Wikipedia as written for a middle school reading level. Understanding
the Bible is not so much a question of difficulty as it is of interest and knowing how to unlock its meaning. This book hopes to
show you how to unlock both the Bible's meaning and the real
joy that will accrue to you from a very personal encounter with
God's Word.

---

6   McDowell, Josh, *Evidence That Demands a Verdict, Volume 1*, (1990), p. ix,
    Here's Life Publishers, San Bernadino, CA
7   *English Bible Translation Comparison* (2006) http://www.ibs.org/Bibles/
    translations/#KJV, citing Comfort, Philip W., *The Complete Guide to Bible
    Versions*, pp. 48-49, 75-81, Wheaton: Tyndale, 1991, International Bible So-
    ciety, Colorado Springs, CO.

Can Everyone Understand Alike?

Realizing it is written at a level even an adolescent can understand may cause us to quickly answer that all can understand it alike. Yet many good and sincere people throughout denominational Christianity believe it cannot be understood alike by all. Why? What evidence do they have?

Well, one evidence is that there are now over 34,000 denominations of Christianity and the number of new ones is growing at the rate of 270 – 300 per year.[8] There were only a few dozen when I was a boy. The dramatic increase in the number of denominations could be an argument of itself that we cannot understand Scripture alike. Of course, there are other plausible reasons for such division: carelessness with God's message, failure to submit to God's will, leaders with another agenda besides making disciples of the Lord, placing the traditions of men over the Word of the Father, different views of the authority of God's Word, etc.

Many today actually believe that everyone is entitled to his own understanding, his own "truth," as it were. This may be a product of the humanistic belief that each one is entitled to go his or her way, that is, to believe one's own thing. Or perhaps it partly stems from the charismatic movement within Christianity, which holds that the follower of Christ is miraculously or directly guided by the Holy Spirit. It is claimed that the apostle Paul taught this when he prayed that "the God of our Lord Jesus Christ, the Father of glory, may give to you the spirit of wisdom and revelation in the knowledge of Him, the eyes of your understanding being enlightened;…" (Ephesians 1:17, 18) The fact is, the passage does not support the notion that each one is entitled to his or her own understanding. Nor does it say that the Holy Spirit will

---

8   Ostling, Richard N., Researcher tabulates world's believers, Associated Press, 19 May 2001, Salt Lake Tribune cites 2001 edition of Barrett's Encyclopedia which counts 33,830 Christian denominations, the number continuing to grow by 270 – 300 denominations per year.

reveal the knowledge of God directly. Many passages speak to the contrary. Paul said very clearly that faith – our understanding and conviction – comes by hearing the Word of God (Romans 10:17). He claimed by inspiration that there is only one truth, one faith (Ephesians 4:5), which cannot be acquired by prayer or other means. It is a pragmatic process that involves study of the Word.

Can everyone understand God's Word alike? The Bible affirms that all can. Paul said so clearly when he taught that God revealed to him the mystery of salvation in Christ Jesus, and he wrote it down for us to read (Ephesians 3:1-7). The apostle said, "He made known to me the mystery (as I have briefly written already, by which when you read, you may understand my knowledge in the mystery of Christ),…" (Ephesians 3:3, 4) Paul said this despite the fact that some of his writings are more difficult to understand than other passages, and Peter warned that "untaught and un-stable people twist to their own destruction" Paul's words as well as all Scripture (2 Peter 3:15, 16).

Even the cases of conversion presented in the book of Acts prove that all can and must understand alike. On the occasion of the first gospel sermon, the apostle Peter explained to a multi-tude who believed why they should repent and be baptized (Acts 2:14-39). Those who gladly received his word and were baptized numbered about 3,000 souls (Acts 2:41). Why did the rest not also obey? Was it because they didn't understand Peter's message? Of course, not! They didn't believe it enough. It wasn't a question of understanding then, and it is not now. It is a question of whether or not people want to humbly submit to just what the Word says, or they want to twist and distort it to fit their own concept of what would please God.

Why Not Leave Theology to Theologians?

There is a popular belief in denominational Christianity that the Bible message can be divided into two groups: *ethics* and *theology*

– ethics having to do with how to live as a Christian and theology dealing with matters of salvation, organization and work of the church, etc. This seems to some a convenient way to have unity throughout the broad community of Christianity yet still maintain the distinction of denominational difference. The idea is that we can unite in our belief that Jesus is the risen Christ, but cling to our favorite means of being saved and worshiping the Lord.

In a similar vein, some have divided New Testament teaching into *gospel* and *doctrine*. The gospel, it is said, is the good news of Christ: His death, burial, resurrection and appearance. Doctrine is, on the other hand, all of the teaching that resulted from that good news: how one is saved, the nature of acceptable worship, and the rest of the teachings in the epistles. Similarly, this view leads some to conclude that belief in Christ's resurrection is sufficient to unite us in Christ, and doctrine is that which we necessarily will understand and practice differently.

Both means of compartmentalizing the message of Christ offer to some the opportunity to move responsibility for understanding the "weightier, more divisive matters" of Scripture to those with theological credentials. If they cannot agree on the nature and purpose of baptism, it is reasoned, how can we who are less trained expect to understand?

Separating *the faith* (Jude 3) into compartments for the sake of ecumenism in the midst of denominational division is, to this writer's mind, a failure to handle God's Word correctly (2 Timothy 2:15). The apostle Paul seems to use *gospel* and *doctrine* interchangeably when he writes to Timothy, "…if there is any other thing that is contrary to sound doctrine, according to the glorious gospel of the blessed God which was committed to my trust." (1 Timothy 1:10, 11) When he warned the Galatians against "a different gospel," (Galatians 1:6-9) surely he was warning against turning from any part of the true faith in Christ, not only belief in His resurrection from the dead. Separating Christian ethics from theology is, at best, equally tenuous. How does one distinguish?

The two are **intrinsically** interwoven. Faith in Christ is all about faith that prompts action: behavior toward God and one another, in other words, ethics and theology all mixed up together in our daily walk and worship.

I fear that those who try to shift responsibility for understanding God's will to others, no matter how learned, are in for a rude awakening at the judgment bar. Where will the experts be when God calls you to answer for your faith? Even if they are close at hand, who is to say which ones have the truth? They cannot agree, and the disagreement among them is increasing at an alarming rate. The only sensible answer is your own diligent study of God's Word. You can understand it, and God expects you to.

Can't Someone Else Do It For Me?

Salvation is a very personal thing. The knowledge which is prerequisite to salvation cannot be accrued for you by someone else. In fact, useful understanding of anything is very personal. To illustrate, try learning a new software application. You can read about it, even play with it, but you will not fully grasp it until you are required to use it to accomplish some series of tasks, that is, use it productively. Then and only then you will come to know it and with practice become comfortable in your knowledge.

If understanding is going to empower you to do something consequential, it first must be made a part of your personal storehouse of knowledge; the facts must be known and accepted by you, its principles must become your convictions, the attitudes it encourages must find a home in your consciousness, and the motivations it provides must be intrinsic, that is, they must spring from within, from your heart. For as a person thinks, so is that person (Proverbs 23:7).

Chapter 1 Discussion

1. Have you had any formal training in how to study? If so, please describe it.

2. What is the Bible? What makes it special?

3. Of all the things that the Bible claims for itself, what is the one thing that has the most value for you? Why?

4. Name at least three other things the Bible claims for itself.

5. Name some groups that claim the Bibles we use have been corrupted and therefore untrustworthy as the inspired words of God.

6. How would you answer them?

7. In twenty-five words or less describe what we gain by studying the Bible. Put as many different benefits into your description as possible.

8. Can everyone understand the Bible alike? Why or why not?

9. Why must our interest in Bible study be intrinsic? In other words, what is there about salvation that makes it so personal?

Chapter 1 Discussion

Why Should I Study?

What's all the fuss about?

But it's so much work, and who cares anyway?

Why study is a basic question, and one that may seem so self-evident that we should not even discuss it. You've heard it said countless times by the preacher, your Bible class teacher, maybe your parents. Study the Bible! Study to complete your lesson for the next class period. Study to know more about God. Study. Study. Study. The sad fact is that very few, even among God's people, do much studying of God's Word for themselves, even though they are continually hearing that they should. Why is that? Should we just accept that most will continue to get all that they know about the Bible from those who teach them from the pulpit and rostrum?

If most are learning something from those who teach, what's all the fuss about? The fact is, somehow we need to find the motivation to study for ourselves. Why should you study? Well, there are many reasons. You already know several, but let's review why every one of us should study for ourselves.

Reasons to Study the Bible

Study to Know the Truth

Here is a grand reason to study. Jesus said, "And you shall know the truth, and the truth shall make you free." (John 8:32) Ignorance enslaves. Worse, the Bible says that sin is transgression of God's law (1 John 3:4), and the wages or payment for sin is death (Romans 6:23). Did you know that truth can set you free from sin and death? It can, and the fact is that there is nothing else that can do that. "You shall know the truth, and the truth shall make you free." This alone is reason enough to study, and unless you study for yourself, how would you know that what you are learning is the truth?

Study to Increase Faith

The Bible says faith comes by hearing the Word of God (Romans 10:17). If you are a child of God, you should realize the importance of strong faith. If you are not yet saved, you will never receive and enjoy the blessing of God's saving mercy without first becoming an obedient believer. That process requires learning some fundamental things about Christ, who He is and what He has done for you and me. As you learn and come to believe the things that you study, convictions will be formed within, convictions which will constrain you to become a disciple of Jesus and make you want to follow Him. Why, even the word "disciple" means "learner," one who embraces the teaching of another and then spreads that word to others.

The apostle Paul wrote very interesting instructions to Timothy, a young man who had decided to become a disciple of Jesus and share his faith with others. He said, "Be diligent to present yourself approved to God, a worker who does not need to be ashamed, rightly dividing the word of truth." (2 Timothy 2:15) The King James Version of this verse begins with "Study to shew thyself approved…" Be diligent is the more understandable translation of the two, but study is still involved. Did you notice that if you are to be approved of God as a worker who has no reason to be ashamed, you must be able to rightly divide the Word of truth? That means dissecting it into its component parts, knowing how to apply what to whom. We will discuss all of this later, but for now, please understand that individual study is necessary if one is to be in a successful relationship with God.

Study to Please God

Throughout the Bible, from the beginning to the end, emphasis is placed upon knowing the Word of God. In the Garden of Eden, it is obvious that God was displeased because Adam and Eve ignored His command not to eat of the tree of knowledge of good and evil. God challenged them about whom they had listened to besides Him, and showed them plainly that they had disobeyed His command (Genesis 3:11, 17). Among the last few words of the Bible is a warning that there will be sad consequences for anyone who adds to or takes away from the words of that book (Revelation 22:18, 19). Early and often in the history of God's people He promised to bless and keep them if they knew and kept His commands (Deuteronomy 7:12-16). The New Testament is no less emphatic than the Old Testament about the need to know and obey God's will. The apostle Paul affirmed that knowing God's Word and walking according to His commandments pleases God (1 Thessalonians 4:1, 2).

Study to Experience the Joy of Discovery

I have used the word "study" frequently in this book, and will continue to do so even though the word itself may carry a negative connotation for many. If you have negative thoughts about studying, I want to confront that feeling head on. Why? Because study is not negative! It is a joyous endeavor, and if you have not yet known the joy that comes from studying, from discovering new ideas and new ways of doing things, from unlocking the mysteries of a previously unknown realm, you have missed something wonderful. I hope I can show you how to tap the joy of study for yourself.

At the beginning, you may consider everything about Bible study to be tedious work and totally devoid of fun. Please keep an open mind, apply yourself to the things we will discuss, and allow yourself to experience the shear joy of discovering the new concepts and principles that God would have you know. As a place to begin, consider this principle that Jesus taught: "…where your treasure is, there your heart will be also." (Matthew 6:21) Jesus said this after giving the admonition that we should lay up treasures in heaven rather than on earth (Matthew 6:19-20). Let me suggest, however, that this principle is actually true in regard to any treasure we may have, wherever we may put it. As an illustration, if you invested all of your money in a particular stock, you would watch its performance daily, maybe check on it several times a day, to gauge its performance. Where your treasure is, there will be your heart, your emotions, also. Also, if a young man sees an attractive young woman and begins to invest his time, money and energies in wooing her, his interest and fondness for her will grow. Placing one's time, resources and thoughts in a particular cause or project will increase interest in that project more and more; its value to the investor will grow. Because of this principle, Jesus said we should invest in heaven. One of the ways you can do that is to spend your time, resources and energy in Bible study. If you do that with a good, positive attitude, I guarantee that you will begin to enjoy study of the Bible. You will discover the joy of learning. And if you go on to share with others the knowledge you acquire, you will experience the joy of teaching, a different and worthwhile joy of its own.

Study to Change Behavior

James, the brother of Jesus, said, "But be doers of the word, and not hearers only, deceiving yourselves." (James 1:22) James understood that knowledge just for the sake of knowledge is devoid of its real value. The true worth of knowing is in putting what you know to use. God made us for a glorious purpose. He placed us here for a reason. Fundamental to why we are here is growing in knowledge that changes us to be more like Him. It is our goal, our true purpose for existing. The apostle Paul tells us that followers of Jesus have citizenship in heaven, and that when this life is over all of those who have been faithful in the Lord will be transformed that we may be conformed to His glorious body (Philippians 3:20, 21). Actually, our lives should be looked at as a process of change by which we are conformed day by day into the image of Christ (2 Corinthians 3:18). Paul warned "…do not be conformed to this world, but be transformed by the renewing of your mind…" (Romans 12:2)

Of this you can be certain: if you make no effort to change your life for the better, you will be pushed and shoved and shaped by the world into the kind of person the world wants you to be. On the other hand, if you renew your mind by regular, systematic and directed study of God's will, and you put the things you learn into practice, you will be transforming your life into the godly creature that God had in mind when He gave you life and being. Study to become godlier. There is no more worthy reason to study. Always remember: life should be a journey between who you think you are and who God wants you to be. And God asks nothing more of you than that which you, with His help, can achieve.

Study to Teach Others

Study is all about knowing Jesus and becoming like Him. Jesus was a teacher. It is impossible to be like the Master without teaching others in some capacity. Of course, not all are teachers at the same level, but all can teach if they prepare themselves with proper study. The expected process of growth in faith demands that we use our knowledge instructing others (Hebrews 5:12-14). Paul instructed Timothy to teach others who in turn would teach

Study to Change Behavior

others, etc. (2 Timothy 2:2) Without such a process, all we know of Christianity and Christians would die out in a few generations. God wants all Christians to teach others so that the message of salvation will reach every generation for as long as the world stands.

Study to Live Forever

The apostle Peter points us to the Word of God, which if obeyed, will purify our souls (1 Peter 1:22). We can trust it to provide for our needs throughout this life and the one after because it is incorruptible, and it lives and abides forever (1 Peter 1:23-25). James agrees with Peter when he declares that we should "...lay aside all filthiness and overflow of wickedness, and receive with meekness the implanted word, which is able to save your souls." (James 1:21)

Is Study Worthy Work Or Drudgery?

To the one who says that personal study is work, I must say, "You're right!" But there is a difference between that which takes effort to produce worthwhile results and that which simply takes effort. Bible study done right is a joyous work; it is not at all drudgery. From beginning to end, it is a rewarding journey.

In this chapter, we have noticed several benefits of study. They far outweigh any expenditure of time or energy. Paul puts things in perspective very well when he speaks of the difficulties and burdens of this life as a "light affliction, which is but for a moment" and is producing for us "a far more exceeding and eternal weight of glory." (1 Corinthians 4:17)

Chapter 2 Discussion

1. What will happen to you if you know the truth? Explain what that means.

2. How does study of God's Word increase faith?

3. Identify a case in the Bible of someone pleasing God by obeying His Word, and then explain the situation.

4. Identify a case of someone displeasing God by disobeying His Word and explain what happened.

5. How important is teaching others about Jesus and His way of salvation?

6. List some things about faith in Christ that you can teach right now.

7. Circle each of the following which will continue forever, that is, will be in heaven throughout eternity: temptation – faith – hope – love – God's Word. If possible, support your answer with Scripture.

8. What joy is there in work? Be prepared to discuss the types of work in which you find joy and describe the joy you find.

Study What?

Does it really make a difference?

How to choose a topic.

Choosing what you will study is critically important to whether or not you will finish the study. Pick something that has value for you, something you need to know. Learning what interests you, satisfies a personal need, or provides some other kind of personal value is much easier than trying to learn what offers you no immediate personal benefit.

Of course, there are many things in Scripture that one might study with profit. A study may have immediate profit in terms of what you are facing or doing in life at the moment. Or, the profit may be less direct providing backdrop knowledge that will help in later studies. In this chapter we will consider some studies which you may find profitable. Our purpose will be to not only describe the study but indicate what specific profit it may offer.

The Covenants

Throughout history, God made different covenants with mankind and especially with His chosen people, the descendants of Abraham. The first of these were the covenants, or agreements, God made with the first husband and wife when He joined them together and with all people after the flood when He promised not to ever again destroy the earth by water (Genesis 2:22-24; 9:8-17). There were other covenants made with His people later on, but there are two we must understand correctly if we are to handle God's Word properly. They are what we call the Old and New Covenants. It is vitally important that you understand these, because they represent the two major law systems governing God's people since the formation of the nation of Israel. Reaching the correct conclusions in any Bible study largely depends upon a correct background understanding of these two covenants.

The Law of Moses was given to the fledgling nation of Israel as the first covenant law system, which all of God's people were under uniformly. Prior to that, God dealt directly with heads of families. Paul described that first national covenant, or Mosaical Law including the Ten Commandments, as a schoolmaster to bring God's people to Christ (Galatians 3:24, 25). This old covenant, contained in the Old Testament, is spoken of as being replaced by a new and better covenant in Christ Jesus, a covenant presented in the New Testament (Hebrews 8:7-13). Hebrews quotes from Jeremiah the promise God made to His people hundreds of years earlier that He would make a new covenant with His people because the first was not faultless (Hebrews 8:7-9).

Can you appreciate the importance of understanding these two covenants and their differences? Many today who profess belief in Jesus consider the Old Testament law to be equally binding upon them with the New. Such a view misunderstands the two covenants, their purposes and their place in the scheme of God's redemptive plan. In Bible times, people did not live under two law systems at the same time, nor do we. To illustrate, the old English law system contained in the document known as the Magna Carta was binding upon those who lived in England from the 13th to the 19th century. It had a great influence in the forming of the United States Constitution and Bill of Rights. Many of our laws were born of the Magna Carta. We can understand our law system better by studying that old system, but its value for us stops there. United States citizens do not answer to the Magna Carta, rather we live under the current laws of our country derived from our own constitution.

In a similar way, the New Covenant is based in the Old, but we do not live under that Old Covenant. Studying the Old Testament helps us know God better, what He wants of humankind, and how He dealt with His people. In it are great examples of faith, which serve to encourage and strengthen us. Still, its authority has passed. Does this mean we do not live under the Ten Commandment Law given Moses? That's right, though all of it is repeated in the New Covenant with the sole exception of the command to keep the Sabbath Day holy.[1] The Hebrews writer affirmed that Jesus is "Mediator of a better covenant, which is established on better promises." (Hebrews 8:6) A Bible student cannot properly handle the Word of God without understanding the covenant under which he or she lives.

The Dispensations

To understand the place of these covenants in the context of the whole Bible you should know that from the Creation until the end of time the dealings of God with mankind can be divided into three periods, generally referred to as *dispensations*. These are —

---

1 Jenkins, Ferrell, *The Theme of the Bible* (1993), p. 71, Florida College Bookstore, Temple Terrace, FL. Jenkins presents a chart in which "...the ten commandments are listed from Exodus 20:3-17. The second column cites the references where the same teaching is found in the new covenant." Passages listed are Acts 14:15, 17; 1 Thess. 1:9; Acts 17; 1 Jn. 5:21; Jas. 5:12; Eph. 6:1-2; Rom. 13:9; 1 Cor. 6:9; Eph. 4:26; Col. 3:9; and Col. 3:5.

1. Patriarchal Dispensation – From Creation until the giving of God's law to Moses on Mount Sinai (Exodus 19:1ff), during which time He dealt with people through the heads of families, the patriarchs.

2. Mosaical Dispensation – From giving of the law to Moses on Mount Sinai until Christ's death on the cross (Matthew 5:17, 18; Galatians 3:19-25; Colossians 2:13, 14).

3. Christian Dispensation – From the death of Christ until now and into the future until He comes again. This covenant is called a "better covenant" with "better promises." (Hebrews 8:6-13) In this "law of liberty" (James 1:25) we find freedom from sins. Paul admonishes to "stand fast therefore in the liberty by which Christ has made us free, and do not be entangled again with a yoke of bondage... You have become estranged from Christ, you who attempt to be justified by law; you have fallen from grace." (Galatians 5:1-4) Paul's instruction is to stand fast in the New Covenant and not go back to the Old.

It is vitally important that you keep the events and especially the commands of God in their proper dispensation. We live under the rule of Jesus Christ, and are not accountable to Moses' laws.

Our Bibles are divided into two sections: Old and New Testaments. You'll remember that the Old is a collection of 39 books and the New includes 27 books. One would suspect from the names Old and New Testament that the books in the Old relate to the Old Law given to Moses and the books in the New relate to Christ's covenant. Such a suspicion is largely but not exactly true. Actually, the record of God's dealings with the patriarchs is also included in the books of the Old Testament, in the early part, and the first four books of the New Testament tell of the life of Christ who lived until His death under the Old Covenant. So, the New Covenant under which we live began toward the end of the four gospel books. Keeping in mind the dispensations and how your study relates to the two major covenants will be a substantial boost toward correctly understanding God's message.

Historical Periods

Though we live in the New Testament dispensation, the history given throughout the Bible of how God has dealt with mankind is critically important to developing our faith. About the old Scriptures, the apostle Paul said, "For whatever things were written before were written for our learning, that we through the patience and comfort of the scriptures might have hope." (Romans 14:4) Learning the major periods in the history of God's people – the period before the flood, the patriarchal period after the flood, the exodus, the period of the judges, the United Kingdom, and the Divided Kingdom – will help you ground your faith in Jesus Christ. An added practical benefit will be an historical context into which you can fit all of the Bible stories and events you will study over time. Your overall understanding of the Bible will be improved. Remember, the Bible is not just a collection of sixty-six books, it is one book.

Prophecy

Prophecy of the Bible is rich with proofs that God is who He claimed to be, that His Word is unerring and is to be believed as unchanging truth, and that Jesus Christ did come as the Divine Son of God in human flesh.

In addition to a great many correctly predicted events surrounding the rise and fall of nations and their rulers, there are over three hundred prophecies in the Old Testament pointing to our Lord's coming and dying. Some are broad and sweeping; others are detailed and seemingly insignificant. Hundreds of years before His birth, the prophets accurately described facts relating to His forerunner, His birth and early years, His mission and office, His miracles and preaching, His betrayal and persecution, His death and burial, and His resurrection and ascension. For example, David spoke of the soldiers dividing Christ's garments a thousand years before it happened (Psalm 22:18). All the prophecies about Christ, both small and great, were fulfilled just as predicted. The smallest detail came to pass.

What is the real significance of so many fulfilled prophecies? Mathematicians have calculated the odds of only *eight* prophecies being accurately fulfilled in one man as 1 in 100,000,000, 000,000,000. That alone would be compelling evidence, but there's more. The odds of *forty-eight* predictions about the life and death of Jesus actually coming true have been calculated as 1 in 10 to the 157th power. How many is that? It has been said that if you had 10^{157} silver dollars, you could cover the state of Texas layer by layer to the height of two feet. Suppose one of those coins was marked and the whole pile was stirred up. Could you find the marked one? Now, if that seems impossible, remember, those are the odds of only forty-eight predictions coming true. Add to that the odds of over *250 additional* prophecies of Jesus the Christ being fulfilled! In the face of such evidence, how can anyone reject the Savior?

Need more? There is a lot more – prophecies of places, times, battles, people and natural disasters – more than enough to attest to the complete credibility of Scripture. The Bible is, without doubt, the divinely spoken Word of God.

As you study, please keep in mind that prophecy is both *predictive* and *instructive*. Including prophecy in your study plans will strengthen your conviction that God is and that His Son is who He claimed to be.

Poetry

More than one third of the Old Testament was written in poetic form. The books of poetry – Job, Psalms, Proverbs, Ecclesiastes and Lamentations – offer a special opportunity for Bible study. God knows that we are creatures with emotions, so He made liberal use of poetry because poetry speaks more directly to the emotions of mankind than any other kind of writing.

God used biographical writing, historical record, doctrinal dissertation, prophetic proclamations and poetic symbolism to get his message across. Consequently, it is wise to recognize the type of writing being studied, and when analyzing one of the Hebrew books of poetry, to be aware of common characteristics of the style. Parallelism, a key feature of Hebrew poetry, is discussed in detail in Chapter 16.

Characters

Character studies are a rich and rewarding way to learn. The Bible is virtually filled to overflowing with colorful characters who, by their life experiences, teach us some of the most valuable lessons of love, faith and persistence to be learned. Pick a character, analyze what the record says about him or her, and then using what you learn write a description of the character, i.e., a character sketch. In other words, what did the character do and why? What lead him or her up to the time recorded, what events unfolded around or where precipitated by the character and what were the consequences of the actions taken, or of the character's failure to act?

One of your assignments at the conclusion of this chapter will be to create a character sketch for a Biblical character of your choosing.

Books

A study of a Biblical book can be one of the most profitable ways to spend your study time. Such a study might properly be called an expository study, a study in which the meaning of the text is exposed, usually verse by verse. Of course, chapters can be studied in this same way, however, as noted below, chapters cannot always be relied on as a proper division of textual thought.

Characters and Books

Books of the Bible were generally written in different styles for different purposes. The authors wrote from different cultural backgrounds and experiences. The Bible affirms that Almighty God inspired all Scripture (Timothy 3:16), but he used men to write down His thoughts. God didn't simply plant an idea in the writer's head and set him free to expand it on his own terms. Rather, the Greek word (*theopneustos*) translated "inspired" means "God breathed."[2] God literally breathed out the words that flowed from the writers' pens. The apostle Paul, who was inspired by God to write most of the New Testament books, said this of the process: "Now we have received, not the spirit of the world, but the Spirit who is from God, that we might know the things that have been freely given to us by God. These things we also speak, not in words which man's wisdom teaches but which the Holy Spirit teaches, comparing spiritual things with spiritual." (1 Corinthians 2:12, 13) Word upon word, it all came from God.

Chapters and Verses

Chapters and verses are a useful means of breaking up Biblical text into more manageable chunks. We read a chapter or two using the chapter breaks to mark our place or we refer to chapters and verses to provide a convenient way to locate passages. Perhaps we have become so accustomed to these divisions that we think of them as divinely inspired separations, just as holy as the words themselves. They are not. The inspired writers wrote without dividing the text into chapters. Paul wrote all sixteen chapters of the first letter to the church at Corinth in one continuous letter with no breaks. Matthew wrote all twenty-eight chapters of his gospel as one document without divisions. So it is with each of the books of the Bible.

---

2   Vine, W. E., Unger, Merrill F., and White, William, Jr., *Vine's Complete Expository Dictionary of Old and New Testament Words*, (1985), see "inspiration of God, inspired of God" on p. 328 of NT section, Thomas Nelson, Inc., Nashville, Tennessee.

Chapters and Verses

It was almost twelve hundred years later (1205) when a man named Stephen Langton, a professor in Paris who later became Archbishop of Canterbury, divided the books of the Bible into chapters. He first put these into a Vulgate edition of the Bible, and the Jews later used them in the Hebrew Old Testament in 1330. By the 1400s, Langton's chapter divisions had found their way into Greek manuscripts of the New Testament, and a printed version first appeared in 1516. Within Langton's chapter divisions, Robert Stephanus, a Parisian book printer, added the verse divisions we have today.[3]

I am glad these men did this work. Chapter and verse divisions have helped me remember where important passages are located, and the overall task of reading one of the longer books of the Bible without chapter breaks would become more difficult. It is usually helpful to break large projects into smaller, more manageable tasks.

While chapters and verses are a blessing, a caution must be sounded. The inspired writer's thought does not come to a conclusion or even a pause at the end of these man-made divisions. When studying his message, remember to follow the thought right through the end of a chapter into the next, if necessary, and to read sentences without concern for division into verses.

Sentences

Words often have different meanings depending upon how they are used. For example, consider uses of the word "church." Speaking of what God did with Christ, Paul wrote, "And He put all things under His feet, and gave Him to be head over all things to the church, which is His body, the fullness of Him who fills all in all." (Ephesians 1:22, 23) In another place Paul wrote, "…Aquila

---

3 For material on the history of the modern chapter and verse divisions see the article in *Die Religion in der Geschichte und der Gegenwart* (3rd ed.), III, 1141 f., and the literature cited there.

and Priscilla greet you heartily in the Lord, with the church that is in their house." (1 Corinthians 16:19) The word church (Greek *ekklesia* meaning a calling out of)[4] is the same in both sentences, but it is obvious that it means different things. The church meeting in a house was a local assembly of Christians who met together for work and worship in the Lord's name. Such a small group is properly called a church – a local church. But in the former reference, Jesus is said to be head over all the church. This must certainly refer to all Christians of all times and places – the church in the universal sense. By the way, the Bible never speaks of a building as "the church."

Until we see a word used in the context of a full sentence, we cannot know its true meaning. How words are used to form sentences – whether sentences of instruction, inquiry, declaration, etc. – is an important consideration when studying God's Word.

Words

We commonly speak of studying God's Word, and should recognize what that means – a study of words. Later, we will discuss studying the scriptural writings in their original context, but for now please take note of the fact that everything written in the Bible was written long before now in another culture and in a language other than English. If we want to know the mind of God on important matters such as why we are here and where we are going, we must consider the message He gave in the way He gave it. It doesn't mean we have to become experts in Hebrew and Greek, but it does mean we must be concerned about the meaning of words as used in the time the Scriptures were written.

I believe "baptism" is an important Biblical word, which God chose to have His inspired writers use several times in its vari-

---

4   Vine, W. E., Unger, Merrill F., and White, William, Jr., *Vine's Complete Expository Dictionary of Old and New Testament Words*, (1985), see "assembly" on p. 42 of NT section, Thomas Nelson, Inc., Nashville, Tennessee.

ous forms. Like many words do, "baptism" and "baptize" have changed in usage over the centuries since New Testament times. Today, an English dictionary might define the word "baptism" as "the religious rite of sprinkling water onto a person's forehead or of immersion in water,…"[5] In the first century, Jesus and His disciples went out to "baptizō," the Greek word for the act of dipping or immersing in water.[6] Unlike today, "baptize" (baptizō) was an everyday, household word used by women when they baptized a piece of cloth in a vat of dye in order to completely change the cloth's color. It might also have been used by a sailor telling about his ship baptizing (sinking beneath the water) in the bay. A New Testament Christian would not have understood if you used the word to indicate sprinkling or pouring. The baptism of Jesus by John the Baptist has often been represented in film by a scene in which John is pouring water from a vase over the head of Jesus. Such depiction is foreign to the first century meaning of the word, and therefore, to the message that God was giving to man when He had the inspired writers use the word.

Remember: the rich blessings imbedded in God's Word can be unlocked only by correctly understanding each word He used. To learn what a Biblical word meant in the time it was used by the writer, turn to a Hebrew or Greek lexicon. It also helps to consider how the word is used in various Scriptures. When you are trying to study all of the occurrences of a certain word in Scripture, a concordance will be helpful. We will discuss concordances and lexicons more in Chapter 6.

Topics

Studying Biblical topics is a common approach to Bible study. There is great value in locating all the Bible says on a particular

5   McKean, Erin, *The New Oxford American Dictionary, Second Edition* (2005), p. 128, Oxford University Press, Inc., New York, New York.

6   Vine, W. E., Unger, Merrill F., and White, William, Jr., *Vine's Complete Expository Dictionary of Old and New Testament Words*, (1985), see "baptism, baptist, baptize" on p. 50 of NT section

subject to understand it thoroughly. You might profitably study such topics as the church, baptism, salvation, faith, gospel, anger, marriage, communication, or any number of other topics.

A topical study is often a good way to answer questions you may have, perhaps a question about marriage, or God's mercy, or the second coming of Christ. These are all good topical studies. By the way, since a topical study cannot always be confined to a single word, you may find a topical bible more useful than a concordance of words because it will identify verses that relate to the topic even though the single word best describing the topic is not in the passage. We will discuss topical bibles more in Chapter 6.

How Do I Choose?

When choosing what to study, remember that staying in the game until the end is crucial if you are going to be a successful student. Pick something that interests you, but by all means something that you need, something that will benefit you and make the expenditure of time and energy worthwhile. If you have questions, mount a study that will provide you the answers you need. If you know that your understanding of historical periods is shallow, and by understanding them more you will strengthen your grasp of the Bible as a whole, spend some time building in your mind an historical timeline of the Bible. If you are not in a saving relationship with Jesus Christ, by all means put salvation at the head of your study list, and go at it!

There may be friends or members of your family who have been urging you to become a Christian. Doing it for their sake is not the best reason. Study the evidence. Investigate God, the Creator of all things and the Promiser of salvation. Consider Jesus and His claims. Weigh the value of eternal salvation against what the world offers. If, after honestly evaluating all of the evidence you are still not convinced, do not repent. God's promise of eternal life is to those who are convinced, those who believe sufficiently to turn from the world to the Lord and obey His commands. Obedience without first believing is meaningless.

Back to the point of what to choose for study. At the end of the day, your study needs to be beneficial to you in order to keep you motivated enough to finish.

Chapter 3 Discussion

1. Of what benefit is studying covenant periods of the Bible?

2. What reasons might one have for studying a Biblical topic? Give an example.

3. What might be a good reason to study the gospel of John?

4. Chose any Old Testament character – male or female, godly or ungodly – and write out all you can learn about that character. Write a story about them in your own words paying particular attention to their background, what made them act as they did, and how the consequences of their actions affected them and others.

5. In Chapter 10 you will be asked to choose a personal Bible study project to complete as you work through the remaining chapters. At this time, select a couple of things you might study profitably. List them here, and give two or three reasons why you made your choices. (These will be only possible choices for your later study project.)

Chapter 3 Discussion

Motivating Yourself 4

How can I keep myself in the game?

Introspection: What motivates me?

Motivating oneself to stay in the game of learning can be a problem. Of course, some students are just naturally motivated from within. They love to learn new things. Others depend upon outsiders to keep them moving. It has long been true that many classroom students expect, or perhaps need, the teacher to motivate them to learn. Research at the University of Michigan indicates "Effective learning in the classroom depends on the teacher's ability to maintain the interest that brought students to the course in the first place."[1] While the instructor may be willing to supply their need, it is unreasonable to expect any teacher to be able to motivate every student. In typical schools, there are other factors that assist teachers in keeping students moving through the material. One of these is the school's system of grading. It provides an obvi-

---

1 Ericksen, S. C. *"The Lecture." Memo to the Faculty, no. 60,* (1978), Ann Arbor: Center for Research on Teaching and Learning, University of Michigan, Ann Arbor Michigan.

ous, even public, means of measuring student progress against course content and comparing them with their peers. Desiring respect from their peers may also keep some from doing very poorly. In any case, students who leave high school for the university may find that these outside factors do not have as much impact on their progress because everything is less personal. In college, students are expected to keep up with the agenda on their own. Of course, mom and dad have to be answered to if they are paying the bills; consequently, they also serve as motivators. All of these outside factors, and others not named, can be placed in a category called *extrinsic* motivation, they are from the outside, or external.

Thankfully, some students don't need such outside inspiration. They are naturally interested in learning, and have an innate ability to motivate self. Whatever attitudes and natural desires drive them can be classed *intrinsic*. That is, of or relating to the nature of oneself. It is by far the very best type of motivation. Students who can cultivate within themselves convictions and attitudes that will intrinsically motivate them will get much more out of study, will do much better making the journey of life, and will have a whole lot more fun doing it. How to intrinsically motivate self is a vitally important subject to consider, especially as you engage in individual, self-directed study.

That is really a main focus of this book. What has been and will be said about motivation is true for any kind of study – school, work, recreation – and is certainly true for study of the Bible. Every disciple of Jesus must be able and willing to engage in individual, self-directed study in order to grow in faith and become like Jesus Christ. While the matters discussed in this book will help a classroom student, our focus is primarily on the self-directed student. In the area of self-study, a lack of sufficient motivation to see a project through to completion will eventually destroy the prospect of any real learning. So how can one motivate self?

Factors That Motivate

It would be nice if there were a simple strategy for self-motivation that would work for all, but there is not. There are many factors that affect a student's desire to learn, and not all learners are motivated by the same things.[2] There has been some research done to identify the key factors that enhance a student's self-motivation.[3] Some of these are:

o   Subject material in which the student can find personal meaning and value

o   An open and positive attitude toward the study

o   Study tasks that challenge but are not too difficult

o   Frequent, positive feedback confirming the student can complete the course of study successfully

o   A feeling that the student is a valued member of a learning community

Let's spend a few minutes considering each of these.

Studying That Which Has Personal Value

Studies have shown that university students are more highly motivated when the class they attend meets the personal needs for which they enrolled in the course.[4] Needs vary by the individual.

---

2   Bligh, D. A. *What's the Use of Learning?* Devon, England: Teaching Services Centre, University of Exeter, 1971, and Sass, E. J., *Motivation in the College Classroom: What Students Tell Us* (1989),Teaching of Psychology, 16(2), 86-88.

3   Lowman, J. *Mastering the Techniques of Teaching.* San Francisco: Josey-Bass, 1984; Lucas, A. F. *Using Psychological Models to Understand Student Motivation,* In M. D. Svinicki (ed.), *The Changing Face of College Teaching. New Directions for Teaching and Learning, no. 42.* San Francisco: Josey-Bass, 1990; Weinhert, F. E., and Kluwe, R. H. *Metacognition, Motivation and Understanding.* Hillsdale, N. J.: Erlbaum, 1987; and Bligh, D. A. *What's the Use of Learning?* Devon, England: Teaching Services Centre, University of Exeter, 1971.

4   McMillan, J. H., and Forsyth, D. R., *What Theories of Motivation Say About Why Learners Learn.* In R. J. Menges and M. D. Svinicki (eds.), *College Teaching: From Theory to Practice. New Directions for Teaching and Learning, no. 45.* San Francisco: Jossey-Bass, 1991.

The student may want to earn a degree, qualify for a certain job, complete some task, acquire a new skill, or just have a new experience. Or maybe completing the course represents simply meeting a challenge head on and succeeding. Whatever the need, a student is more likely to stay with a study that addresses some personal need.

Surely the same is true for those who study independently and must rely on themselves for motivation. Asking, "What should I study?" gets to the heart of the issue. More, why should I study this subject at this time? What will I get out of it? Of what value is it to me? How does this study I have chosen address my personal needs?

Such questions bring us face to face with the issue of true need. Perhaps it would be worthwhile to consider whether your perception of need is a reflection of your true need? A personal illustration may help. When my wife and I moved to Prague in 1992 to teach the Bible, I met many Czechs who knew nothing of Jesus Christ, or the Bible for that matter. Under Communist rule for fifty years, they came for study with me largely out of curiosity – curiosity about Americans and the Bible as a book of literature. Since they knew little or nothing of Christ and what He had done for them, they didn't feel a need to learn about salvation. In fact, several told me that though they had lived under Communism, a godless philosophy, for decades, that system had lost its captive power. Now they were free, and did not need a Savior.

Having long believed that when I study the Bible with someone it is best to start where they are, I began by asking where they wanted to start. Almost always the answer was, "Why, in the beginning, of course. Where else do you start with a book?" Their perception of their need was very different from what I knew their need to be. They needed desperately to cultivate a saving faith, but they felt only a need to satisfy curiosity about the book and its teacher.

The question is what is *your* need? What is your *real* need? Do you need to know the Savior? Or are you in a saving relationship with the Lord and need to know more about His cause, what He has ordained for His church, how to carry the gospel message to a lost soul, how to control your temper, or who the Lord will approve for you to marry. Perhaps you need to know what the unvarnished Word of God says without the filter of a denominational creed that you may have been raised by or may now dominate your thinking. The list of possible needs is long because the Bible provides everything necessary for living life. Your needs are not the same as mine. You are the best one to determine your need…if you are honest with yourself and the Lord. Choosing what you really need to study and what will provide for you the greatest value will of itself serve as a powerful motivator to keep you moving through your study project to reap its benefits.

Keeping An Open Positive Attitude

Keeping an open and positive attitude is necessary to learning and to being motivated in the process of learning. Study is about seeking to know the truth more perfectly. A closed mind will never find the truth. Be open to learning. Be open to new ideas. In fact, your mind should be so open that even ideas and convictions that you have long held should be open to challenge. Suppose what you have long believed is wrong. Suppose your greatest need is to change old familiar notions for those based on truth. Bible study especially needs this kind of openness lest we fail to grasp what God would have us to know and do.

Set aside any negatives about the study and about yourself. If they represent things in your life that need to be changed to please God, don't forget about them. They must be changed, but looking for the positives and concentrating on them is often the better way to correct that which is negative. Through it all, it is crucial that you maintain a positive attitude, an attitude that says you can learn what you need to know and change what needs to be changed. The fact is you can! The apostle Paul said so when he instructed us to bring "every thought into captivity to the obedience of Christ." (2 Corinthians 10:5) Again, Paul said "whatever things are noble, whatever things are just, whatever things are pure, whatever things are lovely, whatever things are of good report, if there is any virtue and if there is anything praiseworthy – meditate on these things." (Philippians 4:8) If you fill your mind with positive thoughts, there will be no room for the negative. If you open your mind to receive what the Lord's written Word will say to you, your learning will be profitable, and if your learning is profitable, it will be fun.

A follower of Jesus Christ is never justified in saying, "I can't!" Paul eradicated that excuse when he wrote, "No temptation has overtaken you except such as is common to man; but God is faithful, who will not allow you to be tempted beyond what you are able, but with the temptation will also make the way of escape, that you may be able to bear it." (1 Corinthians 10:13) There are four positive promises in his inspired statement:

1. No obstacle you face is unique to you; others have faced it before.

2. God will not allow you to be tempted beyond the faith and strength you have to resist the temptation.

3. God is always faithful, that is, He is always trustworthy. His way is right, always. Given the circumstances, another way may appear okay or even best and the majority may be choosing another way, but God and His way can be trusted.

4. God will *always* provide for you a way of escape, a path of godly living through or around every temptation to sin.

Defining Tasks That Challenge — Not Too Much

If you learn at all, you will be charting new waters of understanding. Setting goals that will stretch you, but are realistically achievable is an important ingredient in the process. Clearly define the end result that you hope to achieve by your study. What do you expect to get out of the effort? What value will you derive? With this clearly in mind, look at how you can break the study into logical chunks.

While it is important to have an overall goal for your study, your total project should be broken into smaller study tasks. Each task should be small enough to complete in a reasonable single study session, and each should have its own mini-goal. It is easier to manage and succeed at small tasks than large ones, and if each task has its own measurable goal, stated in specific terms, you will know without doubt when you have finished and will be able to determine how well you did. Reward yourself with a break or a snack, something small but enjoyable. After the first few tasks with a string of successes behind, you will find tackling each new task more enjoyable and your learning will increase.

Frequent, Positive Feedback

What you expect of yourself in each of these tasks should be realistic. Failure to attain your goals will serve only to disappoint and frustrate you. Nothing will dampen your motivation faster. On the other hand, you can powerfully motivate yourself if you have several opportunities to succeed as you progress from the beginning of your project to the end. You can assure this kind of motivation by building into your project plateaus of success, points along the journey that you are certain you can reach. To develop the drive to complete your project in a good way, you must believe that you *can* succeed. The best way to do this is to build in early opportunities for success.

A motivated student needs frequent positive feedback about progress toward a predetermined goal and about how well the work is being done. There should be rewards for good work as each task is completed, and though the rewards do not have to be large, they should be immediate and positive. Both positive and negative comments motivate, but research consistently indicates that students are more dramatically motivated by positive feedback and indications of success.[5]

While each task should be structured so you can successfully complete it, it must also be challenging. If it is too easy, you will not learn much by finishing it and you will not enjoy the feeling of accomplishment that comes from having completed something that has challenged your abilities.

Being a Valued Part of a Learning Community

Feeling an important part of a learning community is more natural to a classroom environment, but not as readily apparent when the student is studying alone on a project selected to meet individual needs. Still, as disciples of Jesus Christ we must realize we are, in fact, part of a learning community even when learning alone. More than that, an important part. Think about it. In Christ, we are a spiritual family bound together in love and a common desire to learn more about the Savior and grow a little more in His image day by day.

Though you study independently of the group, your increasing knowledge and the godly behavior it invokes will reflect on the group. Your influence will be felt, and there will be opportunities to share your knowledge as you help others along the way of life. As time goes on, your study will help you bear fruits in the form of words of encouragement, deeds of kindness, scriptural lessons you have learned which can be shared, and a life example that will inspire those with whom you relate. The other side of this coin

---

5 Cashin, W. E., *Motivating Students*. Idea Paper, no. 1. Manhattan: Center for Faculty Evaluation and Development in Higher Education, Kansas State University, 1979, and Lucas, A. F., *Using Psychological Models to Understand Student Motivation*. In M. D. Svinicki (ed.), *The Changing Face of College Teaching*. New Directions for Teaching and Learning, no. 42. San Francisco: Josey-Bass, 1990

Being Part of a Learning Community

is that you will benefit from others in the group. You may find in them help with difficult questions. They will encourage you, and you will learn from them lessons that will deepen and enrich your own study.

Finding Your Learning Style

Different people tend to have different preferred ways of learning. These are known as learning styles. Three preferred learning styles often recognized in students are the auditory style, the visual style, and the tactile/kinesthetic style. You would do well to understand these in order to identify your own preferred learning style. If you know the style best suited to you, you can structure your study environment to accommodate that style, improve your learning, and be more inclined to stay motivated throughout the project. There is a chart at the following website that may help you decide what style best fits you:

> http://www.chaminade.org/inspire/learnstl.htm

Are you an auditory learner?

Auditory learners seem to learn best when they can hear the material presented. Do you seem to learn more effectively when someone lectures or when you are listening to a tape or a class discussion? If you are this kind of learner, you can enhance your individual study time by playing to your ears. How? Reading the study text aloud or asking and answering questions of yourself aloud will increase your learning. If there are tapes available on the subject you are studying, use them. You may also find listening to a professional read the Bible text on tape is more effective than simply reading it yourself. Doing so will allow you to concentrate wholly on the sound of the message. If you do this, however, I would advise you follow along in the text visually for its own value of gaining familiarity with Holy Scripture.

Are you a visual learner?

Visual learners learn best when they can see the study material in written words or in charts and diagrams. In classroom sessions, they tend to get more when the teacher liberally uses visual aids such as writing on the board, using working models and overhead projector or PowerPoint images. Do you take notes of lecture material? Do you draw diagrams of ideas and concepts you are trying to understand? If so, you are probably a visual learner.

Visual learners do well to take notes and make charts of that which they study. Converting what you learn into any visual form will lend a hand to your mental process of grasping and retaining new information.

Are you a tactile/kinesthetic learner?

Tactile or kinesthetic learners learn best in a hands-on study environment. They want to explore the physical world around them. If you are this type of learner, you prefer handling things about which you are learning. You probably enjoy courses in which there is a lab or some other kind of working-with-your-hands component. Creating a hands-on environment for individual, self-directed Bible study is more difficult than accommodating auditory and visual learning styles, but it can be done by constructing models and miniature objects depicting the items studied.

The power of combined styles

In an IBM employee training session several years ago, I was shown a chart similar to the one on the next page depicting the general effect of learning styles on retaining understanding of what was studied. While the auditory learner might argue that retention is better over time when the material is heard rather than seen, the overall message of this chart is strong. The more different styles of learning you employ the more effective learning will be. What you see, hear, say and do will stay with you much longer than what you simply see or hear. In addition, understanding will be better. Of course, what this chart reveals about learning is not only logical, it is scriptural. James tells us to be doers of the Word, not just hearers (James 1:22-25), and the Hebrews writer explained to his readers that over the course of time they should have become teachers rather than simply hearers (Hebrews 5:12-14). As hearers only they had continual need of being reminded of the

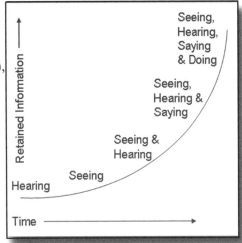

fundamentals of their faith, when they should have been teaching it to others. Doing is an inseparable component of learning in order to grow, and that is what all worthwhile Bible study is about.

Chapter 4 Discussion

1. Describe the difference between intrinsic and extrinsic motivations.

2. Answer each of the following either TRUE or FALSE:

   a. Your attitude toward study has no material effect on whether or not you will finish the study.   _____

   b. It is easier to study a subject you need to know.   _____

   c. Knowing you are a respected member of a group of students makes a study project easier to complete.   _____

   d. It is good practice to break a large study project into smaller, achievable study tasks.   _____

   e. Maintaining a positive "can do" attitude may or may not increase your chances of succeeding.   _____

   f. It usually is wise not to waste time during your study checking on progress.   _____

   g. Extrinsic motivating factors are more effective than any others.   _____

   h. It is usually easy to motivate yourself to study the Bible.   _____

   i. What you are interested in is the best indication of what you need to study.   _____

   j. Putting what you learn to use – that is, doing what you have learned – is the best way to cement your understanding and retain the knowledge.   _____

3. Name the learning styles we have discussed and identify which one you prefer, and why.

4. Suppose you decided to study what the New Testament says about the church, and you scheduled four study sessions over the course of two weeks. For each session, write out a question to serve as a goal for that study period.

5. Are your goals measurable? For each, how will you know when you have satisfied the goal?

6. Now number the questions in the order in which they should be answered, and explain why you ordered them in that way.

Chapter 4 Discussion

Finding a Cool Place

I think I prefer lectures.

Why can't studying always be a team sport?

This book is mainly about independent self-directed Bible study. Still, we each will find ourselves in different settings – worship, Bible classes, spiritual discussions, etc. – where the opportunity to learn presents itself. The diligent Bible student will capitalize on every opportunity to either learn something new or be strengthened in what is already known.

The purpose of this chapter is to consider some ways to glean the most out of every learning situation, no matter where it is found.

How You Study Depends on Where You Study

Centuries ago, Jehovah God told his prophet Jeremiah, "Behold, the days are coming…when I will make a new covenant with the house of Israel and with the house of Judah." (Jeremiah 31:31) Hundreds of years later, the Hebrews writer affirmed that the covenant presented in our New Testament is the very covenant of which Jeremiah spoke. He went on to quote the description of that covenant that God gave Jeremiah: "I will put my laws in their mind and write them on their hearts,…" (Hebrews 8:10) This is a wonderfully encouraging thought for students of the Bible. We can carry His Word with us anywhere and make use of it anytime! In the beautiful first Psalm, David said of this blessing available to everyone who delights in the law of the Lord: "…in his law he meditates day and night (Psalm 1:2).

While we can meditate on it wherever we are, there will be times when we have opportunity to add to the storehouse of knowledge we carry in our minds. Let's consider a few of these opportunities and how we can capitalize on them.

Attending Lectures and Sermons

I know a group of otherwise devout Czech believers in Jesus Christ who meet in small groups weekly to study and discuss God's Word, but who have never seen the need to meet on Sundays for worship and listening to a sermon. They find value in their study sessions, as they should, but would do better if they also met for worship on each first day of the week as Scripture directs (Hebrews 10:24, 25). Most who practice Christianity, however, are regularly in an assembly where someone stands before us to present a lesson from God's Word. Traditionally, at worship or during any Biblical lecture we do not ask questions or otherwise speak. We simply listen.

Sometimes the speaker is not as interesting as we would like, the material is not appealing, or we think we have heard it all before. The mind wanders. It is easier and more enjoyable to think of something else. We may even lull ourselves into believing that thinking about an approaching school event, or that problem at work, or the pressing issue in the family, or the outing we have planned at the lake, or where we should have lunch are all more profitable things to think about. Not so! Such a time is a great opportunity to increase our knowledge of God's Word and sharpen our study skills. How? I'm glad you asked.

The key to listening to someone expound, whether interesting or not, is to involve yourself in the presentation. You can do this a number of ways. Though we will consider study techniques in more depth later, here are a few that fit well a sermon or lecture environment:

1. Look up in your own Bible all of the passages to which the speaker refers. It will keep you involved in what is being said, and will also sharpen your skills in looking up Bible references.

2. Take notes. This is a simple, but very effective study technique that works in a lot of venues. Jot down key words and phrases that are being emphasized. Writing activates the thought process, and what you write is there to be reviewed later.

3. Even more involving than taking notes is the practice of outlining the presentation. This takes a little more skill, but once learned is an invaluable tool for organizing information.

We'll have more on these in Chapter 9.

In An Interactive Classroom

Some classroom teachers tend to lecture most of the time. If your instructor spends a lot of time talking, treat the environment like you would a true lecture or sermon. One advantage to lecturing is more material can be covered in the designated class time. Another is that a few students actually tend to learn better when they are listening. Still, most students learn best when they hear, see, say and do what is being learned. (Do you remember the chart in Chapter 4 depicting this phenomenon?) Herein is the potential value of a classroom.

In an interactive classroom led by an instructor who is skilled in bringing out and directing useful discussion, the motivated student has a rich opportunity to broaden his or her knowledge in a way that may not be possible when studying alone. The value is in the interchange. Ask questions. It has been often said there is no foolish question. That may be true, but in any case, asking your question gives you a chance to put what you are learning into your own words and explore areas for which you need answers. How the teacher and other students respond to your question is a good measure of how well you are grasping the material, or can explain your understanding. Further, the questions asked by others will prompt thoughts you may not find on your own.

During the discussion, take notes. While others are speaking, jot down questions that you may have an opportunity to ask later, or make a note of arguments which would seem to refute what is being said by the group. Through all of it, try to think of Scriptures that relate to what you and others are saying. And don't be shy about asking the teacher and your peers to support what they are saying with a "thus saith the Lord."

You and Yourself Alone

Studying with others is invigorating and provides unique benefits, but the study you do by and for yourself is where the learning rubber meets the road. It is profitable to consider the viewpoints of others, and often someone else will unlock for you some truth you had failed to see by yourself, but at the end of the day Bible study is about building your own faith, forming your own convictions and giving birth to your own godly attitudes.

I hope at this point in this course of study you see clearly the value of charting your own way and achieving your own study goals. I hope you now realize that unless you become personally familiar with the Bible and develop the necessary skills to handle God's Word correctly you will be disappointed in the Day of Judgment.

The Psalmist David said, "Blessed is the man Who walks not in the counsel of the ungodly, Nor stands in the path of sinners, Nor sits in the seat of the scornful; But his delight is in the law of the Lord, And in His law he meditates day and night." (Psalm 1:1, 2)

Learning While Teaching

The Hebrews writer chided Jewish believers for not having left the first principles of faith in Jesus Christ and gone on to be teachers of the Word (Hebrews 5:12-6:3). He explained that they should have grown in maturity to partake of solid spiritual food, a reference to gaining greater knowledge and understanding. Solid food, he said, belongs to those who because of use of the Word are of full age, able to discern both good and evil.

Use is the real key to intimate understanding. Use involves two things: putting into daily practice in your own life what you have learned, and secondly, teaching it to others. Not everyone has to be a classroom teaching or a gospel preacher, but everyone needs to be a teacher. Set the right example before others, to be sure, but do not neglect the verbal teaching of what Jesus is and has done for you. The benefit for you will be great in this life as well as the life to come.

Chapter 5 Discussion

1. What does it mean to have God's law written in your mind and on your heart?

2. Why is this so extremely valuable?

3. Name at least two things you can do during a sermon to help you understand better and retain what you heard.

4. What is the value of an interactive classroom over a traditional lecture?

5. Consider the occasion of Peter's sermon in Acts 2:14-40. Was his presentation a typical sermon of the type we have today?

6. If not, in what way was it different?

7. Would you agree that teaching is one of the best learning tools available? Why or why not?

Using Good Study Aids

You can't build good things without tools.

How to make hard work easy – and profitable!

The more serious you are about learning God's will, the more you will want to add a few key study aids to your library. In this chapter we will consider some of the most useful reference books. Available in digital format for installation on your PC or Mac and in traditional book format for those of us who still enjoy turning pages, these books help you use your time more effectively. Samuel G. Dawson, in his book *How to Study the Bible*, points out, "Since the copyrights have expired on many of these reference works, it is worth our time to search the Web to see if they are available for free."[1]

Of course, it is possible to study your Bible without any of these man made aids, but just as any craftsman without the right tools for the job, you will not be as efficient, or perhaps as accurate.

---

1   Dawson, Samuel G., *How to Study the Bible* (2005), p.187, Gospel Themes Press, Amarillo, Texas.

An Extensive Concordance is Vital

If you use aids at all, this one is vital. In general, a concordance is simply a list of words showing where they are used in a published work, usually with a little of their context. Many Bibles, except the least expensive, have in the back a limited concordance. You can look up a word in the alphabetical listing and find there the verses in which that word is used. While the concordance in the back of your Bible might have some limited value, any serious Bible student – which all faithful disciples of Jesus Christ should be – will have an extensive concordance in which virtually all words in the Bible will be listed.

If you are using a King James Bible, you will find *Strong's Exhaustive Concordance*[2] or *Young's Analytical Concordance*[3] to be extremely useful. If you are using the New International Version, get the *NIV Exhaustive Concordance,*[4] or the *NAS Exhaustive Concordance*[5] if you are using the New American Standard Version.

For years I used Young's with great profit. The publisher of Young's says this about it: "A standard Biblical concordance, Young's casts all words in the Bible into alphabetical order and arranges them under their respective original words. This helps the reader to analyze more accurately the various uses of the original Hebrew and Greek words. Includes over 300,000 Biblical references."

At some point, I changed to Strong's, I suppose mainly because it combines a concordance with Greek and Hebrew lexicons, which my copy of Young's did not do. Strong's Exhaustive Concordance

---

2   Strong, James, *The New Strong's Exhaustive Concordance of the Bible* (1997), Thomas Nelson, Inc., Nashville, Tennessee.

3   Young, Robert, *Young's Analytical Concordance to the Bible* (1984), Hendrickson Publishers, Peabody, Massachusetts.

4   Goodrick, Edward W.; Strong, James; Kohlenberger, John R.; and Kohlenberger, John R, III, *The Strongest NIV Exhaustive Concordance* (2004), Zondervan Publishing, Grand Rapids, Michigan.

5   Zondervan, *The Strongest NAS Exhaustive Concordance* (2004), Zondervan Publishing, Grand Rapids, Michigan.

may be the most complete and easy-to-use. Based upon the King James Version of the Bible, it has with it the lexicons for studying the original languages of the Bible. Beside each verse referenced is a number, which links the use of the word in that verse to the definition of a Hebrew word (for Old Testament words) or a Greek word (for New Testament words) in the back of the book. Any student who uses this book will acquire a clearer understanding of the Word.

For those online, a free lexicon is available at –

http://www.eliyah.com/lexicon.html

In some ways, the online lexicon may be better than the printed version because it is based on later scholarship. After all, more is being learned about the original meaning of words every year. However, do not be discouraged about using slightly older versions. Any differences are probably slight.

Also a Lexicon of Bible Words

As already mentioned, lexicons are dictionaries which give English definitions for Hebrew and Greek words, the predominant original languages of the Bible. If we are to correctly understand the Lord's message to us, we must understand the words He used to convey it.

In addition to Strong's mentioned above, you will want *Vine's Dictionary*.[6] Sam Dawson said, "*Vine's Dictionary* is probably the best for New Testament words. As a matter of fact, if I were on a desert island with only one book in addition to the Bible, I would want a *Vine's*."[7] I agree with Sam, though a good concordance would be sorely missed.

6   Vine, W. E., Unger, Merrill F., and White, William, Jr., *Vine's Complete Expository Dictionary of Old and New Testament Words* (1985), Thomas Nelson, Inc., Nashville, Tennessee.

7   Dawson, Samuel G., *How to Study the Bible* (2005), p.185, Gospel Themes Press, Amarillo, Texas.

Lexicons of Bible Words

Vine points out that when we read the English word "perfect" (Greek *teleios*) its primary meaning is "having reached its end," from *telos*, "finished, complete, perfect."[8] To know that the writer is not saying a thing is without flaw, but that it is complete can make a huge difference in our understanding of a statement like Paul's to the Corinthians about miraculous prophecy: "But when that which is *perfect* has come, then that which is in part will be done away." (1 Corinthians 13:10) Many have supposed that since Paul said "when that which is perfect has come," he was referring to the second coming of Jesus Christ. After all, Christ is the only one who lived perfectly, that is, without sin. But Paul was not referring to Christ, rather he was continuing to speak of prophecy, the subject of that whole context. He was pointing to the cessation of miraculous revelation when the complete message of inspiration would have been delivered, when revelation in parts would be a thing of the past.

New Testament Greek had more than one word to express some concepts for which English has only one. For example, when our New Testament tells us to "love," the writer may have been referring to *agapaō*, acting toward the object of love in a sacrificial, noble way, or he may have had in mind *phileō*, expressing affection or emotional love toward another. The first can be and is commanded, the second cannot be. Actually, the Greeks had two other words for "love:" *storge* and *eros*. The first refers to family love and the second intimate love which may be sexual. Neither of these words is used in the Bible though both types of love are discussed.

There are many words in the Bible like these, which we cannot correctly understand without the aid of a lexicon of the original languages.

---

8   Vine, W. E., Unger, Merrill F., and White, William, Jr., *Vine's Complete Expository Dictionary of Old and New Testament Words* (1985), p. 466-467, Thomas Nelson, Inc., Nashville, Tenn.

A Good English Dictionary

Any authoritative English dictionary will, to some degree, attempt to present in alphabetical order all words that are being or have been used in the English language. The 1933 Preface of the respected Oxford English Dictionary says, "The aim of this Dictionary is to present in alphabetical series the words that have formed the English vocabulary from the time of the earliest records down to the present day (1933 – *parenthetical insertion mine, CB*), with all the relevant facts concerning their form, sense-history, pronunciation, and etymology. It embraces not only the standard language of literature and conversation, whether current at the moment, or obsolete, or archaic, but also the main technical vocabulary, and a large measure of dialectal usage and slang."[9]

A good English dictionary deserves a place on every English speaker's shelves, but a caution is in order. It is not wise to lean on an English dictionary for the definition of Biblical words. That is the purpose of Hebrew and Greek lexicons and other Bible dictionaries.

Topical Bible Dictionaries

Nave's Topical Bible,[10] originally produced by Orville J. Nave as Nave's Topics while he served as a Chaplin in the United States Army, was referred to by the author as "the result of fourteen years of delightful and untiring study of the Word of God." I mention this as testimony to the fact that there is great joy awaiting the one who delves deeply and thoroughly into Scripture. The first publication of Nave's work in the early 1900's included over 20,000 topics and subtopics and 100,000 references to Scripture,

---

9 *The 1933 Preface of the Oxford English Dictionary* as quoted in the article on *Oxford English Dictionary*, by Wikipedia, the Free Encyclopedia, Wikipedia Foundation, Inc., St. Petersburg, Florida, http://en.wikipedia.org/wiki/The_Oxford_English_Dictionary.

10 Nave, Orville J., *Nave's Topical Bible* (1969), Zondervan Publishing, Grand Rapids, Michigan.

and what he did with delight a hundred years ago has helped serve up joy to Bible students ever since. Nave's Topical Bible is available online at http://www.mf.no/bibel/naves.html and several other sites.

Some say *Zondervan's Pictorial Bible Dictionary*[11] is the best-selling one-volume Bible dictionary. There are more than 5,000 entries including discussions of historical, geographical, chronological, and biographical aspects of the Bible. Well endowed with over 700 pictures, Zondervan's may have special appeal to visual learners.

Looking up "Archaeology" in Zondervan's (or other Bible dictionaries) provides insights into how archaeological findings in modern times support Biblical accounts of times and places. Turn to "Marriage" and you will find a comprehensive discussion of its origin, its practice in Biblical times, and teachings of Jesus and the apostles on the subject. Zondervan's Pictorial Bible Dictionary helps you understand the people, places, customs, culture, and events of the Bible. Originally published in 1963, it has since been often reprinted proving its popularity and usefulness.

Another trustworthy dictionary is *Smith's Bible Dictionary*.[12] Over 4,500 subjects and proper names are defined and analyzed with corresponding Scripture references. Smith's dictionary has been used by students of the Bible since its introduction in the 1860's. The publisher has this to say about it: "A classic reference, this comprehensive Bible dictionary provides a wealth of basic background information in a very affordable format. Nelson's edition is revised and edited by F. N. and M. A. Peloubet to be even more applicable to today's Bible student. It includes more than 400 illustrations and special articles in addition to page after page of basic information.

11 Douglas, J. D., and Tenney, Merrill C., *Zondervan's Pictorial Bible Dictionary* (1988 - first published in 1963), Zondervan Publishing House, Grand Rapids, Michigan.

12 Smith, William, *Smith's Bible Dictionary* (2004), Nelson Reference & Electronic Publishing, Nashville, Tennessee.

Topical Bible Dictionaries

"A revision of Smith's classic Bible dictionary, this edition illuminates the original work with the insights of archaeological discoveries. Smith describes the important people and places of the Bible, as well as the major teachings of Scripture. An additional section contains 4,000 questions and answers."

You will find a free online version at –

http://www.ccel.org/ccel/smith_w/Bibledict.toc.html.

Vincent's Word Studies in the New Testament

Vincent's Word Studies,[13] first published in 1887 in four volumes, is a comprehensive study of New Testament vocabulary more in the form of a commentary than a typical lexicon. Vincent discusses subtle differences in meaning between Greek words; comments on the history, derivation, grammar and usage of words; and explains the peculiar characteristics in vocabulary and writing styles of various Bible writers. Vincent provides insight into New Testament word meanings that may be lost in translation from Greek to English.

Bible Atlases

A Bible atlas is primarily a collection of maps and related information pertaining to Bible places normally in Bible times. The Bible is not simply a book full of philosophical ideas and concepts; it is the story of God's people, real people who lived at particular places and at particular times in history. Knowing something of the place and circumstances of God's people will enhance your study of the faith presented in Scripture.

---

13 Vincent, M. R., *Vincent's Word Studies on the New Testament* (1984), Hendrickson Publishers, Peabody, Massachusetts.

Vincent's Word Studies

Many Bibles have a few maps in the back, but a Bible atlas such as *Baker's Bible Atlas*[14] or *Holman's Bible Atlas*[15] offers a more extensive collection of maps along with historical information about the cultural, economic and geopolitical climate of the people.

Bible Encyclopedias

Everyone at some time has used an encyclopedia. A comprehensive encyclopedia includes articles on a wide variety of subjects usually arranged in alphabetical order, a regular who's who and what's what on just about every person, every place, and every thing of significance.

Bible encyclopedias provide a similar wealth of information on every subject Biblical. Perhaps the most widely used, if not the best, is the ISBE (International Standard Bible Encyclopedia[16]) in four volumes. The book jacket on my set has this description of its content: "Representing the meticulous research of hundreds of contributors from many specialized fields of Biblical studies, this edition of ISBE features scholarly excellence..." It is without a doubt one of the most useful sets of books on my shelves. There is a free online version available at –

> http://www.Bible-history.com/isbe/.

Halley's Bible Handbook

In my opinion, *Halley's Bible Handbook*[17] is a "must have." The editorial review on amazon.com says, "Halley's Bible Handbook,

---

14 Pfeiffer, Charles F., *Baker's Bible Atlas* (1961), Baker Book House, Grand Rapids, Michigan.

15 Brisco, Thomas V., *Holman Bible Atlas, A Complete Guide to the Expansive Geography of Biblical History* (1999), B & H Publishing Group.

16 Bromiley, Geoffrey W., General Editor, *The International Standard Bible Encyclopedia* (1979 – First published in 1915 by the Howard-Severence Company, Chicago, Illinois), Wm. B. Eerdmans Publishing Co., Grand Rapids, Mich.

17 Halley, Henry H., *Halley's Bible Handbook* (1965 – 24th edition, 6th printing), Zondervan Publishing, Grand Rapids, Michigan.

the classic layperson's companion text, includes a concise Bible commentary, important discoveries in archaeology, related historical data, church history, maps, and more." In his book on Bible study, Sam Dawson adds his praise: "It's a great little book that gives a breakdown of all the books of the Bible at the chapter level."[18] Halley's is little and concise, but as they say, "Good things come in small packages." Its small size and conciseness are reasons it is so useful. You'll find many occasions to reference it.

The Value of Various Translations

A detailed comparison of the many English translations of the Bible (there are dozens) would be useful, but I will leave that to another time and place. There are, however, some general guidelines for choosing a translation that is reliable. Please be aware that some do not present God's message accurately. Understanding and using these guidelines should provide general insight into the accuracy and trustworthiness of any particular translation.

1. Was the translation done by one man or a scholarly committee? The collaborative work of several scholars is generally imminently more accurate and less biased than the work of one man.

2. Is it possible to know who the translators were? If the translators are kept secret, it is impossible to know their attitude toward the verbal inspiration of Scripture, nor can you know what denominational leanings they may have brought to the project.

3. Were the translators conservative, firmly committed to the inspiration and inerrancy of Scripture? Of course, translators must respect God's verbal inspiration of Biblical writers, and be conservative in their view of the message lest they take undue liberties interpreting its meaning.

---

18 Dawson, Samuel G., *How to Study the Bible* (2005), p. 200, Gospel Themes Press, Amarillo, Texas.

4. Did they attempt to translate the original text literally, or did they easily resort to interpreting Scripture for the sake of modern usage? In other words, what was the purpose of the translators? Fundamentally, there are three approaches to translation: literal, thought-for-thought, and paraphrase. Were the translators trying to produce a literal translation in which the words would closely follow the word order of the original language, were they trying to capture the whole thought with less regard for individual word meanings, or were they producing a paraphrase (Actually, paraphrases are not translations since the "translators" simply rephrase an existing translation without going back to the original language manuscripts.), or something between? Literal translations stay closely with the message but because of word order, grammatical construction and idioms of the original they may be difficult to read. A paraphrase, on the other hand, is very easy to read at the expense of the original meaning. Reliable, useful translations are somewhere between, as close to the literal as possible but still conveying the meaning understandably.

   The English Standard, New American Standard and New King James Versions, though quite readable, are examples of translations that approach the literal. The popular New International Version is more thought-for-thought.

5. Might the translators be prone to denominational biases or would their makeup be a natural check against bias? When there are dozens of translators from different denominations collaborating, there is less chance doctrinal bias will affect the work. Unfortunately, this was truer fifty years ago. In the past few decades, most all denominations have adopted a premillennial view of the kingdom, and many have become more Calvinistic and charismatic. Modern translations may be more prone to biases resulting from such trends in denominational doctrines even though there are a number of translators involved. Having said that, it is interesting to note that the King James Version, the oldest English translation in common use

today, was open to translator bias, not because of doctrinal shift of denominations, but because all of the translators (54) were members of the Church of England.

6. Is the translation easy to understand? There are paraphrased texts available – The Living Bible and The Message are popular examples – which are very easy to understand, but take dangerous liberty with the original meaning. A good translation must be understandable, but readability at the cost of original meaning of God's message is a poor trade.

There are several translations that fair favorably in these tests. Obviously, there are trade-offs. The King James or, as it is called, The Authorized Version (authorized by King James VI of Scotland in 1604, first published in 1611), Revised Version (New Testament in 1881 and full Bible in 1885), American Standard Version (1901), The Revised Standard Version (1952), New American Standard (New Testament in 1963 and full Bible in 1971), New International Version (New Testament in 1973 and full Bible in 1978), New King James (New Testament in 1979 and full Bible in 1982), and English Standard Version (2001) were all done by scholarly committees made up, with the exception of the King James committee, of translators from several denominations.

Before concluding this discussion, let me emphasize the value of having more than one good translation at your disposal. Because the wording will vary slightly one translation to another, your understanding of a passage can be enhanced by considering how different translation committees treated the original text.

Parallel and Interlinear Bibles

These are two unique types of Bibles that bring special benefit to the serious student's studies. An English parallel Bible is the text of two or more English translations of the Bible printed side by side. I have one, the *Comparative Bible, New Testament Edition*,[19]

_____

19 The Comparative Bible, *New Testament Edition* (1969), Royal Publishers, Inc., Nashville, Tenn.

which parallels The King James, The American Standard, The Revised Standard and The Confraternity versions of the New Testament. (The Confraternity is the Catholic Church's version of the Bible.) It is easy to compare different Bible translations with a parallel Bible.

An interlinear Bible is very different. It presents both the original language and a literal English translation together, the English between the lines of the original text. There are several on the market, many with a reference number printed just above or below the original word keying the word to Strong's lexicon. An interlinear translation is very useful for any student seriously interested in pursuing original word meanings without learning the original language.

A Word about Commentaries

There are many good commentaries on the market written by scholarly men well versed in Scripture. They serve as teachers to all those who read their books. While we all need and can benefit from teachers, a loud warning must be sounded about the use of commentaries. A commentary represents one man's view of Scripture. He may be well studied, but no commentator is infallible. What commentators teach seems authoritative if for no other reason than it is written on paper and bound in a book. Beware! If you read a commentary for the purpose of learning the meaning of Scripture, you are laying yourself open to the biases, misunderstandings and dogmatism of which the author might be guilty. Lest you misunderstand, let me hasten to point out that my book is no different. I have tried to avoid dogmatic positions and biases in my thinking. I believe what I teach is not a misunderstanding of God's Word, but I am only a sinful man. You must be as those Berean Jews who "searched the Scriptures daily to find out whether these things were so." (Acts 17:11)

A wise man once reminded me that a study of God's Word is a matter of studying words. It is not about reading books no matter how scholarly. God's Word is what must be learned, not the writings of a man regardless of how many degrees, years of study or books he has to his credit. Do not be intimidated by much learning or a big name. You will not be able to consult a commentator in the Day of Judgment when you give answer for your faith.

Having sounded the caution, I want you to know I believe there is value in good commentaries. They can be very useful tools to aid study, and can give you viewpoints and angles on Scripture that you might never think about yourself. There is a way commentaries can be profitably used. First of all, study God's Word for yourself until you have arrived at your own conclusion about what it means. Afterward, consider what commentaries have to say with the purpose of finding alternative views and supplementary thoughts. If what you read conflicts with your predetermined understanding, go back to the Biblical text to find the truth. Test everything, your own conclusions as well as those of others always remembering that God's Word is the only unchangeable, eternal standard of truth.

At the end of the day, you must remember that commentaries, while useful, must never be blindly followed as the truth – you must do your own study and develop your own faith and not rely on that of others.

Bible Software

Since our topic is aids to Bible study, there must be some discussion of computers and Bible software. These are not necessary to a deep and rich study of God's Word, but for those who are able to use them, they are a blessing. There are many Bible software packages on the market offering a wide range of features and functions at a wide range of prices. Some very robust packages are even free. The price of those for which there is a charge is largely due to royalty fees on certain text modules; therefore, free offerings cannot include these. Some of the more popular Bible translations, for example, are available only in packages for which there is a charge.

Most Biblical texts and useful study aids are available for your computer with full searching and parsing capabilities, and the functionality of software packages continues to increase rapidly. In fact, features, interfaces and speed of operation change so rapidly that comparison is difficult. A few offerings are listed below to give you an idea of what is available. Before you choose, however, it would be wise to Google Bible software and make your own up-to-date comparison.

Commercial Software for PCs and Macs

While some free software systems offer similar or even better language, search, and research capabilities, the following commercial packages may be worth the expense because of their textual content. Owning one of these may be a way of acquiring several thousands of dollars worth of printed material for a fraction of that cost.

Here are a few of the more popular systems presented in alphabetic order. Any comments about them are necessarily dated and not intended to substitute for your own research of current capabilities and user reviews.

o Accordance – Easy-to-use Mac-based system with a powerful interface. Different offerings for different student levels. Puts up to six identical, similar and/or related Bible passages side-by-side for easy reference. Strong user reviews.

o BibleWorks – Features Greek, Hebrew and the Septuagint Bibles with tools designed for close analysis of the original languages. 112 Bible translations available in 30 languages. The interface could be more intuitive. No Mac version.

o Logos – Widely used, robust and sophisticated. You choose modules and libraries that best suit your needs. A cost effective solution. Mac version is due mid-2007.

o PC Study Bible – Powerful and affordable. Includes many conservative commentaries and reference works. A unique feature is their Biblesoft Authoring System, which allows you to write your own study materials and integrate them into the software.

o QuickVerse – Comprehensive solution featuring 23 Bible translations, 58 commentaries, dictionaries, study notes and reading plans plus many other reference works. Uniquely, QuickVerse has an audio feature designed to teach you the correct pronunciation of over 6,000 Bible words.

o SwordSearcher Bible Software – Includes powerful, easy-to-use search tools, 18 Bible translations, several dictionaries, commentaries, and topical guides plus maps and illustrations.

Free Software

You will be pleasantly surprised at the robust search and analysis capabilities available free. There are many offerings, the following three being only a sampling. As indicated before, a software provider who decides to offer a free Bible study application necessarily limits the number of Bible translations and reference works that will be included. Some of the better known works are not royalty free. That said, the free systems should not be easily dismissed. Here are some excellent free systems:

o Davar – Now in final development of some features, this is a powerful search and analysis system with many Greek, Hebrew, Latin and other language lexicons. The library tree makes accessing the array of language sources easy. There is even audio readings of original texts. While not yet as widely known as some others, this solution promises to be a strong contender. Take a look at http://www.davar3.com.

o e-Sword – Includes several free add on Bible versions, dictionaries and comentaries. Its ease of use is enhanced with tutorials, manuals and training demos all free on the e-Sword website: http://www.e-sword.net.

o MacSword – Designed specifically for Mac users. Very versatile, MacSword is an open source application making it compatible with many Bible translations and more than 200 study texts: http://www.macsword.com.

Chapter 6 Discussion

1. For what would you use *Strong's Concordance?*

2. What is the value of a lexicon of Bible words?

3. Explain the danger of using commentaries and identify their value.

4. Describe *Halley's Bible Handbook.*

5. Describe a Bible Atlas.

6. For each below, please indicate whether TRUE or FALSE:

   a. You must know the Hebrew or Greek language to use an interlinear translation. _____

   b. Many Bible dictionaries are really more like Bible encyclopedias than a typical dictionary. _____

   c. A concordance in the back of a good Bible is all the concordance a Bible student needs. _____

   d. The most important thing to look for in a Bible translation is ease of reading. _____

   e. While there may be some minimal value in commentaries, you are better off spending your money on something else. _____

   f. A parallel Bible relates Bible stories in language for kids parallel to the language for adults. _____

   g. Halley's Bible Handbook is a condensed version of the Bible presenting only the essential concepts and principles of Scripture. _____

   h. A literal translation of the original text is difficult to read so it is better to have a paraphrased interpretation which is easier to understand. _____

   i. Many Bible study aids, such as lexicons, concordances and interlinear translations, have been keyed to Strong's original word definitions. _____

7. What is the specific value of a Bible encyclopedia?

Chapter 6 Discussion

Doing Research 7

You've got to be kidding!

I thought research was for nerds.

Doing research may sound ominous to some, but anyone interested in going beyond simply reading God's Word will be involved in spiritual research at one level or another. What is research? Let's start with a somewhat clinical definition from Wikipedia, the online encyclopedia. "Research is often described as an active, diligent, and systematic process of inquiry aimed at discovering, interpreting and revising facts."[1]

Going further with a technical, even somewhat scientific view of research, there are two types: *basic* and *applied*. Wikipedia says, "Basic research (also called *fundamental* or *pure* research) has as its primary objective the advancement of knowledge and the theoretical understanding of the relations among variables... It is *exploratory* and often driven by the researcher's curiosity, interest, or hunch. It is conducted with-

---

1 *Wikipedia, The Free Encyclopedia,* on *Research,* http://en.wikipedia.org/wiki/Figure of speech, The Wikimedia Foundation Inc., St. Petersburg, Florida.

out any practical end in mind, although it may have unexpected results pointing to practical applications. The terms "basic" or "fundamental" indicate that, through theory generation, basic research provides the foundation for further, sometimes applied research."[2] That definition raises the question, "What is applied research?" Again Wikipedia: "Applied research is done to solve specific, practical questions; its primary aim is not to gain knowledge for its own sake. It can be *exploratory*, but is usually *descriptive*. It is almost always done on the basis of basic research."[3]

It should be obvious from these descriptions that both types of research – basic and applied – have their place in Bible study. Most of our study may be more of the applied variety, that is, looking for answers to a particular question or seeking the principles that would guide a particular kind of behavior. However, there is certainly a place for studying rather aimlessly, with no particular goal in mind but to further one's general knowledge of Scripture. Out of such a study many avenues may be uncovered worthy of research for the sake of finding a solution to a particular problem or getting an answer to a question which popped up during the course of basic research. There is a sense in which the open, inquisitive mind-set needed for basic research is useful in all research. We should approach any study with an open mind, not trying to prove a predetermined conclusion.

If you decide to study aimlessly (basic research), please recognize that the tried and true means of motivating your study to a conclusion are less powerful. Remember, motivating yourself is easier when you have a measurable goal in view, and the result at the end of the project holds out real personal value for you.

---

2 Ibid, Under the *Basic Research* heading in the *Research* article.
3 Ibid, Under the *Applied Research* heading in the *Research* article.

The Importance of a Love for Truth

> *John 8:32 – "And you shall know the truth, and the truth shall make you free."*

We should always seek after the truth in all areas of life, not just Biblically; but in no other area does the love for truth hold such great importance and consequence. If we have a love for truth, then our studying will yield great benefit, we will not be swayed by previous thoughts or notions, what everyone else is doing, or what we are told to believe by others. If you have a love for truth, you will be motivated to challenge yourself and study topics just to make sure that what you believe and how you are living your life is in accordance with God's will.

Why Is Personal Research Important?

Why is it so important to seek after the truth for ourselves? The reason is because it is actually very easy to use the Bible to support any doctrine, no matter how bizarre that doctrine may be, simply by using one or two well-chosen passages of Scripture.

For example, I could make an argument that the "eat, drink and be merry" lifestyle is approved by Scripture:

> As the Lord told the parable of the rich man, He said, "And I will say to my soul, 'Soul, you have many goods laid up for many years; take your ease; eat, drink, and be merry.'" (Luke 12:19)

> In Paul's letter to the Corinthians we find, "Let us eat and drink, for tomorrow we die!" (1 Corinthians 15:32)

> And Jesus said, "The Son of Man came eating and drinking,...'" (Matthew 11:19)

By taking Scripture out of context in this way, a few select verses can be fitted together to elevate food and drink to a higher level of importance than warranted. This is obviously a false, distorted belief, but I have some passages which seem to support the view that this lifestyle is scriptural. In a similar way, the Bible can lead readers to many false conclusions if they are not diligently and honestly looking for God's truth.

Using the Right Tools

Trying to screw two pieces of wood together would be pretty hard without any form of screwdriver. With a screwdriver it becomes possible but still requires some time and effort. With a power drill the job can be done easily and quickly with minimal energy. Any craftsman will tell you having the right tools for the job is essential.

So, what 'tools' are useful for research? In the days before the rise of home computers, the main resource for researching a subject was the local library. I remember sitting in the library sifting through a huge pile of books on physics trying in vain to find the elusive needle in the haystack for which I was looking. Why? It was for a college assignment and later for researching historical information related to some Bible study. I usually found the information eventually, but now I can find what I seek in the comfort of my own home in a lot less time using a high speed internet connection and a powerful search engine like Google. We are blessed to live in an age and country where we have such easy access to study materials and a wide range of choices of how to access them. You must simply decide which are the right tools for the job and learn to use them.

Frequently, an effective study of Scripture may involve a variety of tools: topical bible, concordance, dictionary of Old and New Testament words, the Web, some good Bible study software (see more on all of these aids including Bible software in Chapter 6) and any other reference material that may be relevant to that study. You may discover that you get more enjoyment out of flipping the pages of a physical book rather than pointing and clicking on a computer. Whichever tools are the most comfortable for you and in which you find the most benefit will be the right tools for you.

The Value of a Computer

Computers can be fantastic tools if you know how to use them; however, computers are not intelligent. They will not be able to read your mind and magically gather the information you need. If you do not know how to utilize them, they can be frustrating and off-putting. The best way to become proficient at computers is like everything else in life, practice. If you know how to put the computer to work for you, the time it takes to mine information on a subject can be greatly reduced.

Putting the Internet to Work for You

The Internet with the Worldwide Web it supports is like a library with a thousand catalogs none of which contains all the books and all of which classifies the books into different categories. These books move around every night, so the Worldwide Web can be a frustrating place if you do not know how to utilize it properly. On the other hand, it can be a rewarding wealth of information. Most of the reading for this section will be done online via the links below. In the exercises at the end of this chapter you will be asked to use the Google search engine to locate information on the Web. There are other search engines, but arguably none more popular or powerful.

You can make your searches more productive if you know the basics of searching. See Google's advice at –

http://www.google.com/intl/en/help/basics.html

You can go to –

http://www.google.com/intl/en/help/interpret.html

for help interpreting information a Google search returns.

Hints on Electronic Organization

When researching you often come across a large amount of material that you suspect may have value as you progress. If you organize it well, it will aid your future study.

- o Collate your results – copy and paste information (text, photos, and diagrams) from websites into a Word document for reading later. Remember to respect copyright notices.

- o Create a folder in 'My Documents' called something like "Biblical," and then create subfolders within it for each research topic.

- o Bookmark and organize the websites you discover in your 'favorites' (organize into subfolders, etc), create shortcut icons to the most useful websites on your desktop and in your browser toolbar.

A caution about using information found on the Web is in order. Not everything is accurate. Any crackpot who wants to can post on the Web whatever he or she chooses. Pay attention to and check sources. Are they authoritative? Is there corroborating information available?

Staying Focused

Staying focused can be a hard thing to do, especially in your younger years. It was a huge problem for me in school. Sometimes you will find yourself daydreaming and 'zoning out.' Sometimes, something you read while studying will spark your interest, something which has nothing to do with the subject you are dealing with, and thirty minutes later you realize you are now way off track. Maybe something on TV catches your attention and draws you away from your studies, or your friends call you on the phone, etc. Failure to stay focused can result in the study taking a lot longer than planned and may even be the cause of you being sidetracked and losing interest in what you set out to achieve.

To stay focused, make sure you set aside a time block to do your studying. Find a quiet place in the house, turn off the TV, turn off your cell phone, if applicable, and get rid of as many distractions as possible. Be mentally aware of staying on track. If you discover something interesting on another subject while studying, note it down or bookmark the website to come back to it later, and then carry on with the study of your chosen topic. Occasionally review your progress to see if you are still on target for reaching your goal.

A Word about Biases

Many who read this book were raised by Christian parents and grounded in faith from an early age, which is fantastic. You have a huge advantage in scriptural knowledge over someone who may not have cracked open a Bible until in their mid 20's, or later. However, this also means your convictions and opinions on Biblical matters may have been formed largely from what you were taught growing up and did not result from personal study. Keep an open mind when you study and be open to discussion on all Biblical matters. Try to put aside any previous conclusions when you study – it may be harder than you think to truly be "open minded," but your study can yield great results if you are.

Chapter 7 Discussion

1. What is Biblical truth?

2. Can we rely on what our parents and preacher tell us about Scripture to be true? Why, or why not?

3. Whose responsibility is your salvation? In other words, if you are doing something contrary to God's Will, can you justify yourself by saying that was what I was taught by someone else, no matter who or how well-meaning they were? Explain.

4. List six tools that would be useful for Biblical research.

5. Use Google to research the age of the earth and the opposing views of science and Biblical scholars. If you are studying this book in a class, discuss with the group any interesting results you uncovered and what exactly you typed into Google to uncover this information. Note any useful websites you found.

6. How can you help yourself stay focused when researching?

Approaches That Work

Isn't one way as good as another?

How to choose a study method.

There are several ways to approach study of the Bible, each with its own unique value. Which approach you choose depends upon what you are trying to achieve. We will discuss setting study goals in Chapter 10, but for now suffice to say that you will do well to understand your goal first before choosing an approach to the study. Your decision of what to study – the subject of Chapter 3 – and the approach you take go hand in hand. What to study may even dictate the approach you will take. For example, choosing a topic dictates a topical approach. Choosing a book or a passage to study probably means your approach will be largely expository. Though there is a connection between what you study and the approach, they are different and deserve to be considered separately.

You are probably already familiar with various approaches, but it will help to review these before beginning to build a strategy for your next study project.

Reading or Surveying a Book or Period

Simply Reading

Simply reading Scripture has its own special benefit. Reading through the material allows you to get an overall feel for the content. Don't read too quickly, but it is best not to belabor the material. You may find it useful to read aloud. If so, allow your voice to express the passion you find in the text. Stopping along the way for the purpose of analyzing some point is generally unwise. Doing so will undermine the value of reading. If you don't understand everything that is said, that's okay. Make a note to come back later to dig into the material more deeply.

Reading through one of Paul's letters, for example, can give you a feel for the message which may be missed with any other kind of study. Years ago, I decided to start an extensive study of the book of Romans by first reading through the book. I read it through several times and then listened to it on tape a couple of times all with great profit. When the reading and listening were finished there was, of course, much of the message I did not understand well, but I had a good feel for its flow and was able to make a general outline of the letter before digging more deeply into the riches Paul has piled into that book.

Simply reading is generally light and easy by comparison with the deeper study that should follow. Consequently, your mind may tend to wander. Don't let it. If need be, read aloud. Stay focused on what you are reading; read for as much comprehension as possible without getting bogged down in the details.

Surveying a Book or a Period

I highly recommend surveys of Bible books, historical periods, or even a whole testament. It is my firm conviction that every Bible student should survey at least the New Testament if not both Old and New, whether or not the local church includes such a study in their curriculum. The New Testament can be very profitably surveyed in a year by averaging five chapters a week.

This approach involves reading the designated chapters for the week and answering a few questions about the reading. Answering the questions might mean going back over what you read to find the answers, so it is a bit more detailed than simply reading. Surveying the New Testament at the rate suggested will give you an overall understanding of all twenty-seven books in just one year, and you will be amazed at your increased confidence in knowledge of God's Word. Your faith will increase, and you will be well on your way to being prepared to teach those with whom you meet. Not only will you be pleased with yourself, the Lord will be pleased with your attention to His will. Interested?

Sewell Hall, a gospel preacher and diligent student of the Word, has compiled wonderful study guides – *The Old Testament Survey* and *The New Testament Survey* – designed to guide you through a testament in one year. It is a nondenominational collection of unbiased questions that will take you on an exciting journey through the Scriptures surveying New Testament letters in the chronological order of their writing. Also, Darren Brackett, a successful businessman who has delved deeply into Scripture, has an excellent *Old Testament Survey* with a very different approach. You'll find these surveys very useful, and they are free! Simply visit www.clarionword.com/downloads.html to get your copy.

Studying a Topic (Topical)

Learning about some topic involves looking up all of the passages that have something to do with the chosen subject. To find everything will require looking for passages in which any word that describes the topic occurs. For example, suppose you wanted to learn all the Bible had to say about "fellowship." After finding verses like Paul's statement "they gave me and Barnabas the right hand of fellowship" (Galatians 2:9) in which the word "fellowship" occurs, you would want to locate passages that use synonyms of "fellowship" like "The cup of blessing which we bless, is it not the communion of the blood of Christ?" (1 Corinthians 10:16) The word "fellowship" does not appear, but a "communion" is another way of referring to fellowship. Finally, there may be passages in which the idea of fellowship is discussed, but no single word identifies the topic as in the statement "…you are no longer strangers and foreigners, but fellow citizens with the saints and members of the household of God." (Ephesians 2:19) Notice the obvious reference to close sharing together without using the words "fellowship" or "communion."

Studying a Passage (Expository)

As mentioned in Chapter 3, a detailed study of a passage, whether it be a book, chapter or a series of verses, is referred to as an expository study. Such a verse by verse exposition of the text is an effective way of getting to the heart of whatever the passage is teaching. Unfortunately, it seems most sermons heard are topical, not expository. Every study regimen ought to have in it at least an occasional expository study, for there is hardly a richer way to unlock God's treasures.

An expository study can easily be augmented by a topical study within the text as you run across ideas that you would like to develop. Simply locate other Scriptures that teach on that subject, and resume your verse by verse exposition after studying the topic to your satisfaction.

Choosing the Best Approach

Realizing the differences in approaches brings on the question of how to choose. The decision should probably be a function of what interests you, heavily weighted with what you *need* to study. What is it that will provide you the most spiritual benefit? As mentioned in this chapter's introduction, choosing what to study and the approach are closely linked.

If there is a pressing question in your life that needs answer, perhaps you should resolve it with a topical study. If there is someone in your life that you think may end up being your spouse, a critically important question to answer is, "Is this the right person for me for life?" A topical study of marriage will give you a godly basis for answering this question. Do you have a problem with anger and want to know how to correct it? Study what Scripture has to say about anger…or depression. Did you know that the Bible contains very practical advice about dealing with depression?

Are you confused about the relationship between the Old and New Testaments? Again, a topical study can be of assistance; however, if you have more time to devote to the question, surveying the two testaments will put both into perspective for you. Surveying will have the added benefit of giving you an overall historical context for all of the events of the Bible. Having this context will prove to be invaluable as a backdrop for other studies you will pursue in the future.

Though at times our emphasis may seem to be on topical studies, we are never far away from expository study. In many ways, they are two sides of the same coin. During the course of a topical study you may find the need to study several verses surrounding your topic to get the context. In fact, understanding the context is necessary to understanding a verse or even a word in a verse. Contextual study is really another way of referring to an expository study.

Suppose you want to know more about the Savior, so you decide to study the gospel of John. Or you are curious about what Paul wrote to Timothy, so you begin with Paul's first letter to Timothy. In these cases, you will set out on essentially an expository study, that is, starting at the beginning of the book and continuing verse by verse to the end. Along the way, you may run across something that needs more detailed investigation. For example, you read where Jesus said, "And if anyone hears My words and does not believe, I do not judge him; for I did not come to judge the world but to save the world," (John 12:47) and you remember reading earlier that He said, ""For as the Father has life in Himself, so He has granted the Son to have life in Himself, and has given Him authority to execute judgment also, because He is the Son of Man." (John 5:26, 27) The latter comment might cause you to pause and wonder if there is a contradiction, or maybe it is more likely that you misunderstood. How will He execute judgment when He said in a later place that He did not come to judge?

The answer, of course, is not really difficult. He was given the power to execute judgment, but His purpose in coming was not to judge. He came to save. He is the Judge, but that is not the reason He came. While easy to answer, the question might prompt you to pause and spend more time studying the matter of God's judgment before going on with your exposition of John's gospel. The point of this example is to show that topical and expository studies are often used alternatively in a single pursuit of truth.

Whatever other approaches you may choose for various studies, please do not fail to schedule some time to simply read the wonderful word of the Lord. Your life will be richer for it.

Chapter 8 Discussion

1. Read the book of Philippians and write a sentence or two describing the overall impression you have after reading the whole letter.

2. If a friend asked you about Jesus coming back to earth, what approach would most likely yield the information you need? Why?

3. Explain why a concordance may not direct you to all the passages pertaining to a topic you have chosen to study.

4. Make a list of benefits for you that would result from a survey of the New Testament.

5. Which of the four approaches discussed in this chapter appeals to you for your next Bible study?   Why?

"Techniquing" Your Way Through

Technique – technique – who's got the right technique?

Finding your best techniques for understanding and remembering information

There is a variety of techniques from which to choose when approaching study of Scripture. You might want to use several concurrently in a single study. Some you may find useful in virtually every type of study, while others have value only when studying certain topics in certain ways. In this chapter we will look at some techniques the author has found useful, and give some suggestions about when each may best apply.

What has worked well for me may not suit your needs. Each of us is different in how we learn. One may retain information more easily than another and need fewer or different techniques as aids to learning and remembering.

Marking Your Bible

When I first began preparing to teach others the Bible, I made a lot of notes in the margins of my Bible, underlined key verses, and circled words that seemed to deserve emphasis. Then I realized that the blank pages in the front and back of my Bible were an excellent place to list chains of Scriptures relating to important topics. I wrote the word "Faith" and underlined it. Under that heading I listed key verses that taught the importance of faith and how faith is produced. Another heading was "Repentance," and under it were verses about turning from the world to God. Other lists were created for confession, baptism, church, worship, Christ, etc. When I began teaching others, these served as handy reference lists of the verses I would need whenever that topic came up.

If you write in your Bible, some cautions are in order. Be careful that the margins do not become so cluttered and the underlining so prominent that it is difficult to concentrate on God's words. Secondly, if you use colored pens for underlining, be wary of red ink. It may be of the type that does not dry well and continues to bleed across and through the page with time. This can make quite a mess of your Bible. You may find that highlighters are a more effective way of marking verses. Some students have even used different colors to indicate the topic to which a verse relates. Be careful of this technique though. A single verse will often logically fit under more than one topical heading, and your color scheme will begin to break down.

Marking my Bible worked well through the life of two Bibles. There was, however, another downside to the approach. It was traumatic each time a Bible became so worn and its pages so smudged that I had to replace it with a new one. The new Bible had all of the same message that God gave the inspired writers, but what of my notes? I had to start all over. Needless to say, fewer marks were made in the second Bible than in the earlier one. Of course, as time went on my knowledge increased and memory took over for the markings which used to adorn my Bible's pages. Now, I am very thankful there are no notes.

Some may draw up in amazement, even shock, that I would suggest marking in a book which contains God's sacred message. My answer is, the book is not sacred. Though the message it contains is from God, marking the pages does not desecrate the message. If this technique bothers you, by all means do not use it.

Making Notes

Taking notes as you study Biblical text is an easy, yet richly rewarding way to increase learning no matter the method of study you have chosen. Making effective notes involves jotting down key points in a study notebook. Don't write too much. Develop the skill of putting down only that which is necessary to capture a summarized meaning. The process of looking for key words or thoughts is analytical in nature. Your mind is made to quickly sift through details of the material always on the alert for the main thoughts. These form the gist of your notes. Learning to analyze and sift in this way not only sharpens your note taking skills, it improves your ability to grasp the true meaning of a passage.

A good practice is to place the notes you make on the right hand two-thirds or three-fourths of your notebook page. The large left-hand margin is useful for adding action notes, that is, points to research later, related Scriptures that come to mind, questions raised by your textual study, actions you need to take in your life, etc. Your note page might look something like the one on the right.

97

Outlining

Outlining is one of the most beneficial study techniques I have ever used. To outline is to arrange the thoughts of the text logically by placing minor thoughts in proper order beneath the major points they support. The process of analyzing the writer's comments to locate his major and minor points and to understand their proper relationship to each other adds dramatically to your understanding of the material.

Outlining adds value to both topical and expository studies of whatever length, and can be done at various levels of the study material. For example, consider this general outline of the Roman letter, which might result from several readings of the book looking for only major divisions of thought:

ROMANS, THE GOSPEL: RIGHTEOUSNESS BY FAITH

    I. INTRODUCTION

        A. Salutation (1:1-7)

        B. Personal Feelings (1:8-15)

        C. Theme Introduced (1:16,17)

    II. THE GOSPEL PRESENTED

        A. Sin (1:18-3:20)

            1. Sin of Gentiles (1:18-32)

            2. Judgment of Sinners (2:1-16)

            3. Sin of Jews (2:17-3:8)

            4. Universal Nature of Sin (3:9-20)

        B. Salvation (3:21-5:21)

            1. Defined (3:21-31)

            2. Illustrated (4:1-25)

            3. Results Stated (5:1-11)

            4. Adam's Sin to Christ's Redemption (5:12-21)

Outlining

    C. Sanctification (6:1-8:39)

       1. A New Life (6:1-14)

       2. A New Servitude (6:15-23)

       3. A New Relationship (7:1-6)

       4. Prepared by Law (7:7-25)

       5. A New Dominion (8:1-11)

       6. Sons of God (8:12-25)

       7. More Than Conquerors (8:26-39)

III. THE GOSPEL DEFENDED

    A. Paul's Concern for Israel (9:1-5)

    B. Jews' Exclusion Not Inconsistent with Divine Will (9:6-29)

       1. In Promises (9:6-13)

       2. In Justice (9:14-24)

       3. In Prophecy (9:25-29)

    C. Jews Responsible for Their Rejection (9:30-10:21)

       1. Gentiles' Faith Contrasted With Jews' Works (9:30-33)

       2. Jews Given Equal Opportunity (10:1-13)

       3. Faith Comes By Hearing (10:14-21)

    D. Jews Restoration By Faith Promised (11:1-32)

       1. Salvation of Remnant Promised (11:1-10)

       2. Failure of Jews a Blessing to Gentiles (11:11-16)

       3. Warning to Gentiles (11:17-22)

       4. Hope for the Jews (11:23,24)

       5. God's Purpose (11:25-32)

    E. Praise for God's Ways (11:33-36)

IV. THE GOSPEL LIVED

    A. A Christian's Service (12:1-21)

Outlining

        1. To God (12:1-3)

        2. To Church (12:4-8)

        3. To Fellowman (12:9-21)

   B. A Christian's Relationship (13:1-14)

        1. With Government (13:1-7)

        2. With Neighbors (13:8-10)

        3. With Christ (13:11-14)

   C. A Christian's Liberty (14:1-15:7)

        1. Differences in Faith (14:1-12)

        2. Self Denial (14:13-23)

        3. Mutual Helpfulness (15:1,2)

        4. Christ's Example (15:3-7)

   D. Conclusion (15:8-13)

V. CLOSING REMARKS

   A. Personal Feelings (15:14-33)

        1. Paul's Ministry (15:14-21)

        2. Paul's Plans (15:22-29)

        3. Prayers Requested (15:30-33)

   B. Salutations (16:1-23)

        1. A Commendation Offered (16:1,2)

        2. Salutations Made (16:3-16)

        3. A Warning Given (16:17-20)

        4. Greetings Sent (16:21-23)

   C. The Theme Restated (16:25-27)

Suppose, however, your interest motivates you to a more detailed analysis of some passage, say Romans 2:1-20. By comparing the following outline with the Bible, you will notice that in the early part of the outline not every thought of the text is included.

Outlining

Specifically, verses two through five can be easily expanded into much more detail. It is possible for every thought and virtually every word of the inspired text to be organized into an outline, as is shown by the treatment below of verses 17 through 20.

Romans 2:1-20

A. Rebuke of individual hypocrisy (vs. 1)

B. Principles of judgment (vss. 2-16)

    1. According to truth (vs. 2-5)

    2. According to every man's work (vss. 6-10)

    3. According to absolute impartiality (vss. 11-15)

    4. According to the gospel (vs. 16)

C. Sins of the Jews (2:17-3:8)

    1. The Jewish claims (vss. 17-20)

        a. To name

        b. To personal privileges (vss. 17-18)

            1) He rested on the law.

            2) He boasted in God.

            3) He knew God's will.

            4) He approved things excellent.

            5) He was instructed in the law.

        c. To self appointed duties (vss. 19-20a)

            1) A guide to the blind

            2) A light to those in darkness

            3) An instructor of the foolish

            4) A teacher of babes

        d. To special qualifications (vs. 20b)

            1) Having the form of knowledge in the law

            2) Having the form of truth in the law

Outlining

Notice above, the passage that deals with the sins of the Jews runs from Romans 2:17 to 3:8. Not all of these verses are included in our sample outline. There would necessarily be an item 2. and so on following what is shown. Since item 1 under "Sins of the Jews" is titled "The Jewish Claims," can you determine from the Biblical text what item 2 might say?

When you spend the time analyzing a passage sufficiently to divide its thoughts into the logical structure of an outline, you will improve your grasp of the message dramatically.

Grammatical Diagramming

Diagramming of sentences was a skill taught when I was in high school. I don't recall many students who enjoyed it, I suppose because it is a very tedious practice and depends upon knowledge of the grammatical parts of speech – pretty boring stuff for many teenagers. Despite the alleged negatives, diagramming is an effective way of dissecting a sentence to milk the essence of its thought. In the ensuing years since school, I have used that skill only a few times in Bible study. It can be helpful because it forces the student to identify the subject of the sentence, its verb or action, as well as various modifying words and clauses, and then place them into a diagram which clearly shows the relationships among them. Understanding the structure of a sentence enhances understanding of the sentence's meaning.

Diagramming comes in handy when dealing with a sentence that is difficult to understand or is so long as to be confusing, as are some of Paul's sentences. If you would like to learn more about how to diagram sentences, go to this website:

http://www.geocities.com/gene_moutoux/diagrams.htm

Reading and Rehearsing Aloud

Reading aloud improves retention as well as understanding of what you read. This is especially so if you are an auditory learner.[1] Whatever type of learner you are, reading aloud slows down the input of content to your head allowing your brain to process it beyond the auditory level and internalize it to the level of understanding.[2]

Not a good reader? Not to worry; reading is a skill which can be learned. Doing it will improve your ability to do it. If you are a poor reader, you probably have some fear of reading aloud when called upon in class or when with a group of your peers. Wouldn't practice make you feel more comfortable in those circumstances? Surely it would. It's an old saying, but true: practice makes perfect. Practice reading aloud in private during your personal Bible study, and reading aloud in public will get markedly better.

Read with feeling for the message. When you read of Christ cleansing the temple of money changers, feel His indignation (John 2:13-17). Express it as you read. When you read of the mob crying out to Pilate for the crucifixion of Jesus, say it with passion (Mark 15:8-13). Can you feel the edge of Pilate's frustration as he answers their insistent cry, "Why, what evil has He done?" (Mark 15:14) Express it in your voice. Experience the message and it will come alive in your understanding.

For many of the same reasons, rehearsing aloud what you have learned has as much benefit as reading aloud – even more if you are rephrasing the information in your own words.[3] Use your voice to help you improve your learning and increase retention of what you learn.

Reading and Rehearsing Aloud

1   *Auditory Learning* (2003), http://www.cuyamaca.edu/eops/DSPS/resourc-saud.asp, Cuyamaca College, Cajon, California.
2   Sharpe, Wesley Ed.D, *Reading Aloud - Is It Worth It?* (2001), http://www.education-world.com/a_curr/curr213.shtml, Education World, Inc.
3   *Study Skills - Reading Effectiveness*, Sam Houston State University Counseling Center, http://www.shsu.edu/~counsel/hs/studyskills.html#reading.

Writing – Expressing It in Your Own Words

Next to explaining to another person what you have learned, answering their questions and defending your conclusions, I have found no more effective way of learning than to write out in my own words my understanding of the message. You don't have to be an accomplished writer to benefit from this technique, unless you plan to publish what you write to the scrutiny of others. Can you understand your writing? That's all that matters. In fact, the value of this technique is not really in reading what was written, though that is beneficial. The greater value is in the writing itself.

Read a sentence from the Bible and try to express it in your own words. Copying the words and phrases as the inspired writer wrote them is not acceptable. Restate what the author wrote, but in your own words. Include every thought. Then continue with the next sentence. Don't stop at a sentence or two. Do a whole paragraph. It is not really necessary to do it sentence by sentence. In many cases, a whole paragraph can be re-crafted into your words without doing damage to the thought. That, of course, is the goal: to rewrite in your own words the exact thought of the inspired text.

There is value in simply copying the inspired text word for word since it helps to fix God's word in your mind, but the real value of writing comes from reformulating the thought into your own words and writing those words down. Make what you write sensible. Make it as comprehensive as you can. The idea is to reword all of the author's thought, not just a part of it.

Finally, it is good practice to save these writings. What you write becomes a type of personal commentary. Later, after studying other matters, when you revisit this same text, you will find you can deepen your understanding because your general knowledge has increased.

Asking Three Important Questions

There is a technique particularly suited to expository and topical studies that I will describe here. It is easy to learn and use, and I favor it because it focuses on the infallibility of God's Word and reminds us of our responsibility to interpret it correctly. Further, this is a method of study that anyone can master easily and use profitably.

What I call the "Three Questions Technique" is based on what Jesus said to a lawyer who came to test him (Luke 10:25-28). The lawyer asked Jesus what he must do to inherit eternal life. Jesus answered by asking him two questions: "What is written in the law? What is your reading of it?" In these two questions, Jesus pointed him to God's law given through Moses, the law in effect at that time, and then asked how he understood it. God's Word is infallible; a man's understanding is fraught with the possibility of error. The lawyer could have understood it correctly, or he could have understood it incorrectly.

Interestingly, the man answered that the way to inherit eternal life is by loving God above all else and your neighbor as yourself. What is most interesting about this answer is that it is nowhere written in the Mosaic Law. It is written that one should love the Lord with all their heart, soul and strength (Deuteronomy 6:5), but nowhere in that context is loving neighbor or inheriting eternal life mentioned. Loving neighbors as oneself is taught in another book (Leviticus 19:18), but nothing is said there about loving God or about eternal life. The lawyer put together two separate parts of the law – loving God and loving neighbor – and concluded that if one does these he will inherit eternal life. In fact, the question of how to inherit eternal life is nowhere succinctly addressed in the Old Covenant. The lawyer interpreted the law. Jesus went on in that discourse to say, "You have answered rightly; do this and you will live." (Luke 10:28) Of course, when we interpret we can interpret incorrectly. The lawyer didn't. A critical part of the goal we must have for all of our study is to interpret correctly.

I believe that in this discourse between Jesus and the lawyer we have a Divine plan for Bible study. There are three parts: What does God's Word say? What does it mean? And what should I do? An excellent way to study a Bible book is to form three columns in a notebook. Head the first column *What does it say?*, the second *What does it mean?*, and the third *What should I do?* Each day study a verse or two, or perhaps a paragraph of the book. Copy the text you are studying in the first column, and then write out what you think it means in the second. This is your personal commentary of what that verse or section means. Then in the third column, if you need to change something in your life to conform to what you have learned, write it out. It becomes your action list resulting from your study.

What Does It Say?	What Does It Mean?	What Should I Do?
Colossians 3:1 – If then you were raised with Christ, seek those things which are above, where Christ is, sitting at the right hand of God.	Being "raised with Christ" is a reference to coming out of water baptism where we contact the death of Christ and are cleansed by His blood. Only those who believe in the risen Christ and are baptized into Him have a reason to seek heavenly things. (See Romans 6:3-8) Others need to first seek a relationship with Jesus before seeking other heavenly things.	I have been immersed into Christ. Therefore, I am like those to whom Paul wrote on this occasion. This is speaking directly to me. What can I do today to seek those things above where Christ is?
3:2 – Set your mind on things above, not on things of the earth.	Focus on spiritual matters, keep them foremost in mind as much as possible.	I must get back to daily Bible study, and spend more time in prayer, not just at meal times. If I start actively seeking a lost soul to convert this year, the commitment will help me fill my mind with heavenly things.

"Three Questions Technique" from Luke 10:25-28

This is an excellent way to study a book. As an example, consider the letter to the Colossians. It is short (four chapters) but powerful, a book that calls us to change. Start in the beginning and study just a few verses each day using the three question method.

Notice my study example of Colossians chapter 3 on the opposite page. I copied the Biblical text word for word in the first column. There is value in simply copying God's Word. These are the inspired words of Truth, and writing them out may impress that concept more than simply reading them. I may be able to understand them correctly, or maybe not. Whatever I do with them, however I understand them, they are still Truth. They will not bend or change to suit my whims or preferences or my careless treatment of them.

Paul said, "If then you were raised with Christ, seek those things which are above,..." You will see my explanation in the second column that "raised with Christ" means coming out of baptism. The text does not say that. Baptism in not in this verse, nor in the immediate text. This is my potentially fallible understanding of it. To support my understanding, I referenced Romans 6 where Paul says in verse 4, "Therefore we were buried with Him through baptism into death, that just as Christ was raised from the dead by the glory of the Father, even so we also should walk in newness of life." My understanding of this is that just as He was raised, we also must be raised from our watery burial. Verse 5 strengthens my understanding: "For if we have been united together in the likeness of His death, certainly we also shall be in the likeness of His resurrection." Just as He was raised, we are raised from baptism to a new life in Him. This is the basis of my understanding of "raised with Christ" in Colossians 3.1. Could I be mistaken? Yes, but no other passages on baptism refute this position. In fact, many support it. Consequently, at this point of my understanding, I don't believe my interpretation is wrong. So, I moved to the third column to make the application of verse 1 to me.

This three question technique of study is as useful for topical studies as it is for expository. The previous example was expository, while the one on the next page is a section of a topical study on baptism.

What Does It Say?	What Does It Mean?	What To Do?
Romans 6:3-8 – 3 Or do you not know that as many of us as were baptized into Christ Jesus were baptized into His death? **4** Therefore we were buried with Him through baptism into death, that just as Christ was raised from the dead by the glory of the Father, even so we also should walk in newness of life. **5** For if we have been united together in the likeness of His death, certainly we also shall be in the likeness of His resurrection, **6** knowing this, that our old man was crucified with Him, that the body of sin might be done away with, that we should no longer be slaves of sin. **7** For he who has died has been freed from sin. **8** Now if we died with Christ, we believe that we shall also live with Him,….	From the many important lessons in this passage I will try to address only those directly related to baptism. First, baptism is the way we get into, or experience, the death of Christ. There are at least two reasons that this is very important: 1) It is in the death of Christ that we contact the saving power of His shed blood. By it we are justified, or saved (Rom 5:9); brought near to God (Eph 2:13); make peace with God (Col 1:20); are redeemed (1 Pet 1:18, 19; Rev 5:9); cleansed from all sin (1 John 1:7); washed from sins and made white (Rev 1:5; 7:14); and overcome the devil (Rev 12:11). 2) We must taste of His death in order to taste of His resurrection (Rom 6:4, 5). It is in baptism, which is the "likeness of His death", that we crucify our old self with Him. It is at that point that the sins of past life are done away, and we are no longer slaves of "sin leading to death, but of obedience leading to righteousness" (vs. 16). Verse 4 affirms that baptism is a burial into death, "that just as Christ was raised from the dead … we also should walk in newness of life". New life in Christ begins as one rises from the watery grave of baptism. The old life of sin is past, the new life in Christ lies ahead. This is where sins are washed away as those of the Corinthian brethren (1 Cor 6:11). Not by the action of water, but by action of God in response to a good conscience (1 Pet 3:21). Paul's likeness of baptism to the death, burial and resurrection of Christ is in complete harmony with NT Greek meaning of the word *baptizō* (to dip or immerse). This view that baptism is immersion in water and is essential to one's salvation is the only view that fits this passage. There is no other mode or purpose of baptism that comes close.	I have been baptized (immersed) into the death of Christ. Therefore, I have nothing to do regarding this passage but teach baptism this way until someone can show me how to understand this passage more perfectly.

The scope of this study was determined by locating every scriptural reference to the words baptism, baptisms, baptize, baptized, and baptizing in the New Testament. Then each verse was analyzed in the method described above. A portion of that study is presented on the opposing page.

Throughout this book, the value of using questions is mentioned often. Questions are a good way to express measurable goals for your study as discussed in Chapter 4. Chapters 10 and 14 recommend using a variety of questions during the process of interpreting Scripture, and Chapter 10 offers a list of possible questions to use in different situations. The three questions discussed here serve as a framework for your study, but please do not conclude from this discussion that use of these questions is in anyway a substitute for the others. When you are developing an answer to the question What does it mean?, you will find that using a wide array of questions about the text will be an invaluable aid in arriving at the Lord's meaning.

Praying

May I begin this topic by respectfully saying we do not pray enough? If you are an exception and have no need of praying more than you do, my hat is off to you. God bless you. Let that light shine! The rest of us need to follow your example. Tradition says that James, the brother of Jesus and the author of the epistle of James, had calluses on his knees from so many hours in prayer. I recently heard of an elderly man saying he was praying more and more as his life drew near its end. He said he wanted to be certain that God recognized his voice. I like the sentiment though I suspect he knew that God is intimately aware of each of us. Still, our Father wants to hear us pouring out to Him in prayer our hopes and fears, our doubts and confidences, our joys and difficulties, and whatever else is on our hearts. What better reason

Praying

could we have for prayer than a desire to understand His will for us more perfectly?

While it is wise to pray for God's help in understanding His message, we have not, as some have supposed, been guaranteed perfect understanding solely on the basis of prayer. Years ago, I met with a man who began our study with a prayer asking for God's help in reaching an understanding of what we would study. I was willing to amen such a prayer, perhaps not fully understanding what he meant by the help for which he asked. Later, when we disagreed on the meaning of what I thought were plain passages, he said he was certain his understanding was correct. It was so, he said, because he had asked for help and it had been promised by Jesus in John 16:13 that the Holy Spirit would guide us into all truth. The Spirit would not misguide. He also cited Paul's statement to the Ephesians that he prayed for them "that the God of our Lord Jesus Christ, the Father of glory, may give to you the spirit of wisdom and revelation in the knowledge of Him, the eyes of your understanding being enlightened;..." (Ephesians 1:17, 18) My friend's conclusion was that when he prayed for help the Holy Spirit miraculously opened his eyes to the truth, therefore, his understanding was infallible. He could not explain to me why I had a different understanding though I had participated in the same prayer for help.

The fact is, the comment Paul made about understanding being enlightened in no way suggests miraculous intervention. The spirit in the verse is the human spirit, a disposition for understanding. Also, the promise Jesus made that the Holy Spirit would guide into all truth was not made to us. It was made to only the eleven apostles, Judas being absent (John 13:18-30). Notice the context of Jesus' comments. He set the stage for His promise of the Holy Spirit by saying, "These things I have spoken to you while being present with you. But the Helper, the Holy Spirit, whom the Father will send in My name, He will teach you all things, and bring to your remembrance all things that I said to you." (John 14:25,

26) He said those things "...while being present with you." In the following verses, He makes several references to reminding them of things He said to them when He was with them, and to leaving them. Just before restating the promise at John 16:13, Jesus said, "But these things I told you, that when the time comes, you may remember that I told you of them. And these things I did not say to you at the beginning, because I was with you." Then He reiterated and expanded upon the promise of the Holy Spirit's guidance (John 16:7-15). Though I have tried, I cannot find an honest way to apply these words of Jesus to us today. It would violate one of the fundamental rules of correct interpretation of any Biblical text: many things are written *for* us, but not *to* us. Could what my friend did with these Scriptures be one of the reasons there are now thousands of denominations claiming allegiance to Christ with more being added every day?[4]

The process is pragmatic. Paul said faith (understanding and resulting conviction) comes by hearing God's Word (Romans 10:17). Prayer helps, but correct understanding also requires a love of truth, an open mind, and skill in handling His Word correctly (2 Timothy 2:15).

The apostle Paul said, "Pray without ceasing." (1 Thessalonians 5:17) Surely it means be ready to pray on every occasion and for every reason. Pray always that He will help you cultivate a sincere love of truth. Pray before you begin a study session that your mind will be alert and open to the truth, not encumbered by your own biases or those of denominational Christianity around you. Pray to remind yourself of your relationship to Him, the created to the Creator. Pray to humble yourself before His eternal word. Pray when the meaning of a difficult passage seems just out of reach. Pray as you prepare to reach a conclusion from your study. And when you have prayed about all else, get on your knees to

Praying

---

4 Ostling, Richard N., *Researcher tabulates world's believers*, Associated Press, 19 May 2001, Salt Lake Tribune cites 2001 edition of Barrett's Encyclopedia which counts 33,830 Christian denominations, the number continuing to grow by 270 – 300 denominations per year.

thank God for sending His Son to die for us and for sending His Spirit with the message of truth that sets us free.

Meditating

Your mind, of course, is the center of who you are. The wise man, Solomon, said, "For as he thinks in his heart, so is he." (Proverbs 23:7) From ancient times, the heart has been used to represent the mind of man, the seat of thoughts and feelings. Because your mind is at the center of your being and drives your attitudes and your actions, it is imperative that you guard what is in it. What do you think about when your mind is at idle? What type of thoughts "lay upon" your mind? Are they wholesome? Positive? Upbuilding?

The Miriam-Webster Dictionary says to meditate is "to engage in contemplation or reflection…to engage in mental exercise."[5] A regular systematic study of God's Word will provide a wealth of spiritual fodder for exercising your mind. Let righteousness lay upon your mind. Dwell on that which is godly. The apostle Paul admonished, "…whatever things are true, whatever things are noble, whatever things are just, whatever things are pure, whatever things are lovely, whatever things are of good report, if there is any virtue and if there is anything praiseworthy – meditate on these things." (Philippians 4:8) Actively dwelling on the Scriptures you have been studying is an excellent way to follow Paul's instructions.

I believe it was Albert Einstein who said the average person uses only 10% of his or her brain power. Oh, that we might unlock more! The mind is an immeasurable blessing from God. Use it wisely. Review godly concepts while driving, dwell on righteousness while strolling down the lane, turn Scripture over in your mind while waiting for the dentist, and rehearse God's will for your life whenever there is an appropriate lull in your activities.

5 *Miriam-Webster Online Dictionary* entry for *meditate* (2006), Miriam-Webster, Inc., Springfield, Massachusetts.

Memorizing

Memory is not so much lost as hard to find.

Steven Rose

What a maddening thing memory can be, dodging away from you when you're trying to snag it, descending around you like a collapsing tent when you most want to forget it.

Los Angeles Times

Progressive educators call it "drill and kill," but learning poetry by heart empowers kids, according to some. Memorization is something of a lost art. In his article *In Defense of Memorization*, Michael Knox Beran decries the current attitude: "If there's one thing progressive educators don't like, its rote learning. As a result, we now have several generations of Americans who've never memorized much of anything. Even highly educated people in their thirties and forties are often unable to recite half a dozen lines of classic poetry or prose."[6] What difference does it make? Beran argues it makes a huge difference in our society, in who we are. He goes on to give several reasons why students should be taught to memorize and recite poetry and passages of prose. But what about memorizing in connection with Bible study? Is there value? I believe so.

You would do well to have in memory the timeline of Bible history, at least in summary form. As you read or study, you will be able to easily plug characters and events mentioned into their correct historical context. Having major events recorded in the book of Acts, the early history of the church, stored away in your memory is a great help toward understanding the inspired letters and the challenges faced by the early disciples. Committing these things to memory requires conscious memorization.

---

6 Beran, Michael Knox, *In Defense of Memorization* (2004), City Journal at http://www.city-journal.org/html/14_3_defense_memorization.html, The Manhattan Institute, New York.

Another thing I recommend memorizing is the location of key verses and Biblical passages. They must be easy to find in your own study as well as studies with others. Some folks advocate memorizing the verses themselves, word for word. I spent time doing that many years ago, but stopped. I found quoting verses from memory a hindrance in studying with others. I believe it is much wiser to turn pages and read the passage together no matter how familiar the text. I prefer setting an example before a Bible student with which they can identify, an example they can emulate. Besides, focusing attention on the printed Word of God has its own value. That is not to say that memorizing the thoughts and phrases of Scripture and their locations is not good. It is, and I recommend it highly to fuel your own meditation and discussions with others.

If memorization is a lost skill, let's spend some time exploring how to develop it. Your brain has several functions, one of which is to be your storehouse or reservoir of knowledge. That is the function we call memory, an important ingredient of learning. Memorization is not learning, but no learning really takes place without memory. Understanding is what greases the slides. With effort it is possible to remember what you don't understand, but long-term memory is energized when you understand what you store away. When you really understand, memorizing is easy.

Did you know that a strong memory can be developed? Involving yourself completely in the learning process is probably the most important consideration. You must want to learn and you must work at remembering. Though there are dozens of memorization techniques, we will consider only four you may find helpful.

Association

Actually, we remember things by association all the time. If you think of your friend, Joe, you might then remember the last time you were together, his favorite food, his hobby or his family. All of these things might come to mind because those memories are associated with thoughts of him. You probably would not think of a horse unless you know that Joe is fond of horses. Memory by association is natural for us, so why not consciously use it to advantage to remember the things we are learning? Children memorize the names of the apostles and the books of the Bible by singing songs about them. Associating the names with notes of the song's melody eases the pain of memorizing even long lists like the names of sixty-six books of the Bible.

First Letter Cueing

Remembering is the business of digging up what is buried somewhere in your mental storehouse. Cueing, or acrostics, is a way of assisting that process by initially storing away an associated cue along with the data being memorized. It could be a list of words whose first letters spell out something easily remembered like this list:

> **B**lessed
> **I**nformation
> **B**ringing
> **L**ife
> **E**ternal

Or it might be a phrase you create in which the first letter of each word serves as a cue for remembering something. It works best if the cue is funny or ridiculous. For example, you might use the nonsensical phrase "Patriarchs are Mostly Christen" to remember the three dispensations of Bible history: Patriarchal, Mosaical and Christian. Of course, no patriarchs of Bible history were Christians, but that kind of nonsense actually aids memory. Acrostics have been in use to help memory since the time of Christ, and they still work.

Peg Words

Peg words are a good way to remember an ordered list of things such as the names of Israel's kings or the prophets of old in the order they appeared in history. Start with a list of words or images that you can remember, a list that you make up. These are your peg words. Then you peg each thing you want to remember to one of the peg words. Dale Carnegie has used this system of teaching memorization with a list of 21 peg words: 1) Run, 2) Zoo, 3) Tree, 4) Door, 5) Hive, 6) Sick, 7) Heaven, 8) Gate, 9) Wine, 10) Den, 11) Football Eleven, 12) Shelf, 13) Hurting, 14) Sorting, 15) Lifting, 16) Licking, 17) Movie Screen, 18) Waiting, 19) Shining, 20) Horn of Plenty, and 21) Dueling Gun. Each peg image rhymes somewhat with its number, which helps you to remember them in proper sequence. When you have your peg list memorized, the items to be remembered are associated with each of the pegs. For example, for Run visualize a horse running without a rider, but something is on it. That something is the first item in your list to be remembered. Secondly, imagine feeding a monkey at the Zoo; what are you feeding it? The second thing to remember in your list. Thirdly, visualize a Tree being pulled down to the ground. What is doing it? Your third item to remember. Get the idea? The ridiculous images conjured up by this approach actually aid memory.

You don't have to use the same peg word list as Dale Carnegie taught. Make up your own. The system works.

The Method of Loci

The Method of Loci is a memorizing technique that dates back to ancient Greece. It combines organization, visual memory and association, and works well in memorizing unordered events. It can be implemented a number of ways. One is to visualize a house with several rooms in which pieces of furniture are arranged. It should be easy to create such a mental picture; it could even be your own house. The house or a mental picture of any other arranged space combines organization and visual memory to provide a familiar framework in which to associate the people, items or events to be remembered. Simply take a mental trip through the house attaching items to be remembered to pieces of furniture in various rooms. A subsequent journey through the rooms in any order looking at the items of furniture will prompt recall of the associated items.

Memorization Requires Organization

Perhaps you have noticed that in every one of these memorization techniques there is some form of order. Information that is organized is more easily remembered. When you find and understand the logic behind the information, you will find that remembering it is much easier. If the information to be remembered is truly random, then concoct an organization upon which to hang those thoughts as in the Method of Loci.

A Word of Caution

Now that I have come out strongly in favor of memorization, I must emphasize what was said earlier: memorizing is not learning and is no substitute for it. Good memory comes from *comprehension*, not the rote activities many students call "memorization."[7] Never allow yourself to be lulled into the notion that because you have memorized something, you know it.

Review

Most student learn at an early age that review of what they have learned is a good way to retain it, at least until the book report, lab assignment or test is over. It has long been known that most of what high school and college students learn is forgotten soon after the assignment or test in which the knowledge is needed.

Teaching another person, usually not thought of as a means of reviewing what has been studied, is perhaps the most effective

---

7   Dewey, R., *The "6 Hour D" and How to Avoid it* (1997), Available online: http://www.gasou.edu/psychweb/discuss/ch00/6hourd.htm.

learning technique of all. Every use of the knowledge learned is not only review but a blending together of knowledge with the skills required to share it.

The effectiveness of different ways to learn were suggested by D.G. Teichler in 1967.[8] He claimed students learn and retain –

> 10% of what they read;
> 20% of what they hear;
> 30% of what they see;
> 50% of what they both see and hear;
> 70% of what they discuss with people whose opinions they value;
> 80% of what they personally experience; and
> 90% of what they teach to other people.

While the even distribution of Teichler's percentages suggests the numbers are not scientific, his observations seem very logical. They are reminiscent of the IBM study mentioned back in Chapter 4. We retain much more of what we use than what we simply take in.

Of course, Teichler's insight was not really so new when published. The Hebrews writer stated the principle long ago when he chided Hebrew Christians for not growing beyond the need for spiritual milk and becoming teachers of the word: "For though by this time you ought to be teachers,… For everyone who partakes only of milk is unskilled in the word of righteousness, for he is a babe. But solid food belongs to those who are of full age, that is, those who by reason of use have their senses exercised to discern both good and evil." (Hebrews 5:12-14)

8   Treichler, D. G. (1967), *Are you missing the boat in training aids?* Audio-visual Communications, United Business Publications, New York.

Chapter 9 Discussion

1. Name at least two techniques that you can incorporate in your study practices, and tell how they will be useful.

2. Name at least three things that would be good to ask of God in prayer when sitting down to a Bible study session.

3. Jesus taught an important principle in Luke 6:45. Write out the thought of this verse in your own words. Be as complete as possible.

4. What is the value of memorization?

5. What is the value of reading aloud?

6. Considering what Jesus said to the lawyer in Luke 10, what three questions can be a useful guide to Bible study?

7. When is it good to use outlining as a Bible study technique?

8. How is teaching what you learn an important part of the learning process?

Charting Your Own Way

If you fail to plan, you are planning to fail.

Knowing where you are going makes the way clearer,... and more fun!

Every successful business man or woman knows the importance of planning. It has often been truly said, "If you fail to plan, you are planning to fail." We are each on a journey. Life is a series of passages from one station or plateau to another. No one is standing still. You are either expending effort to move ahead in a good direction or carelessly sliding down the slippery slope of futility, failure and disappointment. The difference is in fixing your gaze on a worthwhile destination, charting a good way to go, and setting sail with sufficient effort and determination to successfully reach your goal.

The French writer and aviator Antoine de Saint-Exupery (1900 – 1944) was one of the pioneers of international postal flight in the days when aircraft had few instruments and pilots flew instinctively by "the seat of their pants." He wisely said, "A goal without a plan is just a wish."

Defining Your Purpose

Goal setting

Set a goal, which is another way of saying define your purpose. Wrap your head clearly around what you want to get out of your study, what benefit or value you expect to receive. It could be to find the answer to an important and perplexing question. It could be to prepare yourself to teach a class or an individual in your acquaintance. It could be simply to ratchet your faith up a notch or two as you strive to reach a higher plateau of knowledge in the Lord Jesus. It could be to explore all the evidences for belief in God that have eluded you until now. Maybe it is because you heard the preacher or Bible class teacher explain something in a way that was strange to you, and you want to check it out to see if it is scriptural.

Whatever your purpose, define it clearly. Write out the definition, and then set down on paper how you will know when you have fulfilled that purpose. State your goal in measurable terms. A goal against which progress cannot be measured is no goal at all.

Scoping your project

After defining your purpose, determine the scope of the current study project. If your statement of purpose is fairly specific (what is a husband's role in marriage?), what you will study and the scope of study will be obvious. If your statement of purpose is general (increase faith), you will need to decide the subject and scope of study since any study of the Bible should increase faith.

Daniel H. Burnham (1846 – 1912), an American architect and urban planner who designed several famous buildings, threw up this challenge: "Make no little plans; they have no magic to stir men's blood… Make big plans, aim high in hope and work." While aiming high creates for you a welcome challenge, it is wise not to aim too high. Set realistic goals. Challenge and stretch yourself for sure, but it will be easier to sustain your motivation to finish the project if you are able to actually achieve what you have purposed.

Developing a Strategy

Setting mini-goals

After determining what you will study and the purpose for that study, you need a plan for achieving your goal. The first step in developing a study plan, or strategy, is to set mini-goals. Generally, students want to achieve their final goal in one gigantic step. To be more realistic they probably need to map out at least three intervening steps they will reach along the way to the final goal.[1] Goals should be both positive and specific. Especially the earlier ones should be relatively easy to achieve, thus assuring early success in your endeavor.

It is best to write goals out in a journal or study notebook so they can be easily referred to later. Rather than stating a goal as "Study hard," try something like "read chapter six and answer these questions: Who are the main characters? What did they do that pleased God? What temptations did they face, and how did they overcome them?"[2] Or, "analyze the first ten verses of Galatians 2 and list the three most important points." Well, you get the idea. Be specific and be realistic. State your goals so you can measure progress. When deciding how to state the goals you will have, keep this thought in mind: the best goals are summed up in the thought that goals must be turned into actions.

---

1   *Reaching Learning Goals*, Indiana State University Center for Teaching and Learning (1998), Indiana State University, Terre Haute, Indiana.
2   Ibid

Determining your approach

Next, identify the approach you will take: reading, surveying, studying a topic or exposing the meaning of a passage or a book. The best approach should practically "fall out of" the preceding steps of stating your purpose, scoping the project and setting mini-goals.

Choosing the best study techniques

Having considered several study techniques in the previous chapter it should be clear that some will be more useful than others in a particular kind of study. I have found in expository studies of more difficult passages my learning is greatly improved by outlining the message, but I do not outline every study. The techniques I have found most generally useful are making notes, writing a paragraph or two about what I have learned, frequently reviewing what has been studied, and teaching the material to another. In addition, I cannot emphasize too much the value of using what I have called the three question technique based on the discourse between Christ and the lawyer in Luke 10. Every study, without exception, should include prayer at the beginning, at the end and at any critical point or question between.

The importance of planning

Planning is important, but don't spend too long in doing it. According to the very successful general, George S. Patton (1885 – 1945), "A good plan, violently executed now, is better than a perfect plan next week." If you are uncertain whether or not to spend time planning, another successful general as well as president of the United States, Dwight D. Eisenhower (1890 – 1969), put it into perspective for us: "In preparing for battle I have always found that plans are useless, but planning is indispensable." Planning is useful, but your purpose is to study, not to plan. Start the project. Once into it, don't be afraid to discard your plans if a better course comes to light.

Asking Pertinent Questions

Asking questions is one of the most powerful ways to learn. Every learning strategy should make liberal use of questions. Asking good questions and finding the correct answers will always be profitable work. You'll find that certain questions can serve you well in a variety of studies. Here are some old standbys for your consideration:

When analyzing a passage or book, ask –

Who wrote this, and to whom did he write? What were his circumstances and theirs? Why did he write? Was there a problem that needed correction? Did he write to them at an earlier time or perhaps later, and what changes took place between the writings? Why? Is the teaching here a part of the law under which I live, or was it part of a previous covenant? What should I learn from it, and what should I apply to my life? Remember, what you learn may not apply to you. You may learn from it, but it may be something only they needed to heed. For example, the command to build an ark was made to Noah, not to you or me.

When probing a word meaning, ask –

What is the meaning of this word in the original language? How does the immediate context affect this usage of it? How is this word used in other Scripture? Does the writer express this same thought in different words in another place? Does that have an affect on the meaning here?

When studying a topic, ask –

What word(s) looked up in a concordance would help me locate passages dealing with this topic? What synonyms will help me find more passages on this subject? Will a topical bible help? Have I made a diligent search for everything God has said on this subject before drawing any conclusions about what to believe?

When studying a Bible character, ask –

What does the text tell me about this individual's character, attitude, spirituality, desires, etc.? What events led the character to this place at this time? What is the character doing now? How have past events affected present behavior? What other characters are there in this story and how do they affect the outcome? How is God's hand in the situation? Who is affected by the person's behavior? How? Are the consequences produced by this behavior good or bad? Is the character growing in faith or falling away from the Lord? Why? Why is God pleased, or not?

When drawing conclusions, ask –

Have I approached this study with an open mind? Have I diligently avoided any biases, either mine from past teaching and experience, those of friends and relatives, or those from denominational Christianity? Have I avoided drawing conclusions that contradict plain teaching elsewhere? Have I avoided reaching conclusions based on ambiguous or figurative Scripture? Are the conclusions I have drawn based on the sum total of all that God has said? Is the conclusion inescapable, or is it one of several possibilities? Have I prayed adequately about reaching the right understanding? Have I been truly motivated by a love for truth and a willingness to accept God's Word for what it says regardless of what it might do to my preconceived ideas? Am I willing to accept the truth even though it may cost me the comfort of a long-held conviction? How about if obeying His Word costs me the respect and association of those I love?

Identifying Reasons to Stick With It

It is critical that you keep yourself motivated throughout the project. What value is there in starting and never finishing? You can be certain you will finish successfully by frequently focusing on the good you have accomplished and the value you will receive when the study is completed. Though we discussed self motivation in Chapter 4, the subject may bear another look as we consider identifying reasons to stick with the study.

"Literature on motivation and classroom learning has shown that motivation plays an important role in influencing learning and achievement.[3] If motivated, students tend to approach challenging tasks eagerly, persist in difficulty, and take pleasure in their achievement.[4] Research has also shown that instructional context strongly affects students' motivation. Instructional materials that are challenging, give students choices, and promote perceived autonomy and self-determination can have a positive effect on students' motivation."[5] The keys to motivation according to learning experts are challenging tasks, pleasure in achievement, challenging instructional materials, student choices, personal control and self-determination. All of these are within your grasp. In self-directed study, you do well to incorporate all of the above.

Determine your own goals and chart your own course. Challenge yourself in a positive way, and enjoy the pleasure that waits along the way as you successfully achieve one milestone after another.

3   Min Liu, *Motivating Students Through Problem-based Learning*, The University of Texas at Austin Dept. of Curriculum & Instruction, University of Texas, Austin, Texas citing Ames, C. A. (1990), *Motivation: What teachers need to know*, Teacher College Record, 91(3), p. 409-421; and Dweck, C. S. (1986), *Motivational processes affecting learning*, American Psychologist, 41(10), p. 1040-1048.
4   Ibid, citing Stipek. D. (1993), *Motivation to learn: From theory to practice.* Needham Heights, MA: Allyn & Bacon
5   Ibid, citing Deci, E. L., & Ryan, R. M. (1985), *Intrinsic Motivation and Self-Determination in Human Behavior.* New York: Plenum Press; Hidi, S and Harackiewicz, J. M. (2000), *Motivating the academically unmotivated: A critical issue for the 21st century.* Review of Educational Research, 70(2), p. 151-179

Planning to Review

Identifying reasons for continuing in your learning journey implies that you take time along the way to review where you are, what you have accomplished and the benefits that await if you but continue to pursue your goals.

Periodic review is important. It is the way you know if you are still on plan and moving in the right direction. Have you ever been on a driving trip and failed to pay attention to road signs along the way? A wrong turn unnoticed can result in many miles off course in a relatively short time. Review not only lets you know your progress, it keeps you headed in the right direction as planned. Remember though, the plan with which you started is not sacred. You may find while progressing through your project that your plan requires changing. Do not hesitate to make revisions as needed.

Chapter 10 Discussion

1. Choose a topic or short book of the Bible to study for a continuing project as you progress through this book. This may be one of the choices you made in Chapter 3 or something else altogether. Write your choice here along with a short sentence defining the purpose you have in mind.

2. What benefit do you expect to receive?

3. Break your study project into manageable sessions, each representing thirty to sixty minutes of study time. Identify a measurable goal for each session. For example, if you chose the topic of baptism, you might break the study into three sessions during each of which you will find the answer to a question: 1) What is New Testament baptism?; 2) Who was a candidate for baptism in the days of the apostles?; and 3) What was the purpose of their baptism? You will know when you have achieved your goal for each session when you can write out a comprehensive answer to that session's question. If you choose a short book, a chapter might be a study session, and for each chapter your goal might be to write a brief summary of the author's main points. For your project, define each session and write out the goal for that session.

Session 1:
Goal 1:
Session 2:
Goal 2:
Session 3:
Goal 3:

continued next page

Chapter 10 Discussion

Session 4:
Goal 4:
Session 5:
Goal 5:

4. For at least your first planned session, make a list of questions the answering of which will help you reach your goal for that session.

Context? What's the big deal?

"A text without a context is just a pretext."

The American poet, John Godfrey Saxe (1816-1887), based his poem, *The Blind Men and the Elephant*, on a fable told in India many years ago. Though a familiar tale, I can think of no better way to remind us that forming conclusions from a partial view can result in seriously flawed interpretations. (And I like seeing the whole poem in context.)

Blind Men and the Elephant
by John Godfrey Saxe

It was six men of Indostan
    To learning much inclined,
Who went to see the Elephant
    (Though all of them were blind),
That each by observation
    Might satisfy his mind.

The First approached the Elephant,
    And happening to fall
Against his broad and sturdy side,
    At once began to bawl:
"God bless me! but the Elephant
    Is very like a wall!"

The Second, feeling of the tusk,
    Cried, "Ho! what have we here
So very round and smooth and sharp?
    To me 'tis mighty clear
This wonder of an Elephant
    Is very like a spear!"

The Third approached the animal,
    And happening to take
The squirming trunk within his hands,
    Thus boldly up and spake:
"I see," quoth he, "the Elephant
    Is very like a snake!"

The Fourth reached out an eager hand,
    And felt about the knee.
"What most this wondrous beast is like
    Is mighty plain," quoth he;
" 'Tis clear enough the Elephant
    Is very like a tree!"

The Fifth, who chanced to touch the ear,
    Said: "E'en the blindest man
Can tell what this resembles most;
    Deny the fact who can
This marvel of an Elephant
    Is very like a fan!"

The Sixth no sooner had begun
    About the beast to grope,
Than, seizing on the swinging tail
    That fell within his scope,
"I see," quoth he, "the Elephant
    Is very like a rope!"

And so these men of Indostan
    Disputed loud and long,
Each in his own opinion
    Exceeding stiff and strong,
Though each was partly in the right,
    And all were in the wrong!

Moral:
So oft in theologic wars,
    The disputants, I ween,
Rail on in utter ignorance
    Of what each other mean,
And prate about an Elephant
    Not one of them has seen!

I am afraid that many who profess allegiance to Jesus Christ are doing just what the blind men did though their distorted view of faith in Christ has much more serious consequences than misunderstanding an elephant's anatomy. Surely this approach to Scripture is at least partially responsible for the proliferation of denominations that make up today's world of Christianity.

If we are to honor God and His will at all, it is imperative that we listen to everything He has given on a subject before claiming to know His mind, and it is essential that every separate part of His Word be understood in its proper relationship to all the rest. To do less is to be no smarter than the blind men of Indostan.

An Overall View of the Bible

If we are to have a good understanding of God's message, we must take firm hold of the whole Bible and the kind of language that is used to convey its history, unfold its predictions, declare its commands and impress its promises. We need to feel its poetry and imbibe its wise sayings. There is no other book like it in style and scope, but more than that it has no equal because it is divinely inspired. It is truth – unchangeable, incorruptible and everlasting.

The Bible relates the noble deeds of godly men and women who were willing to sacrifice all for the sake of righteousness, but it also tells of the dastardly deeds of evil persons bent on bringing good people down to unspeakable lows of deceit and destruction. We dare not allow our treatment of it to be haphazard or nonchalant. We cannot afford the consequences of coming away from its study with a distorted or lopsided view. The serious Bible student will be diligent in acquiring a complete and balanced view of its structure, its principles and its truths.

Learning the Context

What is context? The word comes from Middle English meaning "weaving together of words, Latin *contextus* connection of words, coherence."[1] Today we understand "context" to mean "the parts of a discourse that surround a word or passage and can throw light on its meaning."[2] It is impossible to understand anything fully without knowing its context. Can you honestly say you know Mozart's Piano Concerto No. 21 if you have heard only a few notes from the middle? How about Superman (It's Not Easy) from the American Town CD by John Ondrasik and his Five for Fighting? How much of the lyrics do you have to hear before you get Ondrasik's message? Could you understand the workings of an automobile engine by examining a piston? You must consider the whole to understand a part. To do this, study the larger or broader context as well as the immediate context. We will look at a couple of scriptural examples in the next section.

Some professional educators may be overheard referring to the "funnel approach" to learning. This view recognizes the value of learning the general concepts about a subject before moving on

---

1   *Merriam-Webster Online Dictionary*, http://www.m-w.com/dictionary/context, Merriam-Webster, Inc., Springfield, Massachusetts.
2   Ibid

to the details. Just as a funnel's larger end tapers to its smaller, the funnel approach stresses the larger context as a framework within which to understand the parts. The funnel approach makes sense. If you fail to ask who wrote a letter, to whom and why, you will likely misunderstand the message or not understand it as fully as you might otherwise. If you are unaware of what the chapters before and after say, your understanding will be on shaky ground. It makes a difference what period of history is under consideration, and it makes a huge difference which covenant covers the text being studied.

The funnel approach does not preclude starting your study with a verse. Simply back away from the details long enough to get a handle on the context before going further with the study.

The Broad and the Immediate Context

Words have a dictionary meaning, which may include alternate usages or shades of meaning. They take on more precise meaning when placed in sentences, and even more when in the context of a paragraph. Careful scrutiny of the immediate context is important in the process of learning what a passage means. Any passage must be understood in light of what immediately precedes and follows it. No one dips into the middle of a letter or a book and expects to know what that document is about. Neither can we understand a Bible verse without considering its immediate context. An old maxim says, 'A text without a *context* is just a *pretext.*'

As an example, consider what Paul wrote to the Corinthians: "It is good for a man not to touch a woman." (1 Corinthians 7:1) Is Paul saying a man is never to have physical contact with a woman? Of course not. He is referring to sexual contact. How do we know? By the context which is dealing with sexual immorality. (1 Corinthians 5:1-5; 6:9-20; 7:2, 9)

We have another example when Jesus said, "No one comes to Me unless the Father who sent Me draws Him;…" (John 6:44) By itself, this statement has suggested to some that the Father decides who will come to Jesus, excluding others, and exercises some special drawing power upon them, providentially if not miraculously. Some have adopted that position in an effort to strengthen their doctrine of predestination. Reading further indicates otherwise. Jesus went on to say, "It is written in the prophets, 'And they shall all be taught by God.' Therefore, everyone who has heard and learned from the Father comes to Me." (John 6:45) In context, it is obvious Jesus was teaching that the drawing would be done by the Word of the Father and that anyone who learned and obeyed it could come to Him. Often Scripture explains itself if we but keep its teaching in context.

Sometimes, knowledge of a very broad context is necessary for understanding a single verse. For example, a much broader look is required to grasp a statement Joshua made to God's people just before his death: "Therefore it shall come to pass, that as all the good things have come upon you which the Lord your God promised you, so the Lord will bring upon you all harmful things, until He has destroyed you from this good land which the Lord your God has given you." (Joshua 23:15) What good things had come upon them? What were the things God had promised? Without knowing these things we could not possibly understand Joshua's warning in the same way as those who first heard him. Just two chapters earlier we are told "not a word failed of any good thing which the Lord had spoken to the house of Israel. All came to pass." (Joshua 21:45) To what fulfilled promise of God is Joshua referring in both of these statements? Knowing the whole story of the book of Joshua helps answer that. It is the account of Joshua's leading Israel in conquering the land God had promised Abraham way back in Genesis. (Genesis 12:1-3; 15:7-21)

Correctly understanding the land promise given to Abraham, which was fulfilled in Joshua's time depends upon the broader context of several generations of Bible history. About its fulfillment, the divine text says, "All came to pass." Further, a correct understanding of this promise affects an even broader contextual view of the kingdom of God. If all that God had promised Abraham had been fulfilled in Joshua's time, should we now continue to wait for a return to that physical, promised land?

Keep in mind, the individual interpretation of a verse, a passage or a chapter must not contradict a correct understanding of the totality of Scripture. No part stands alone. All parts are bound together, cohesively woven into the whole of God's truth.

The Value of an Historical Timeline

Keeping Bible characters and events in proper perspective becomes much easier when you have a mental timeline of Bible history. Having some idea of dates will be helpful, but it is more important to know the relationship of major periods and events in the history of God's people, that is, a chronological arrangement down through history. What happened first? What happened next? What happened after that? Having this historical context into which you can plug all that you learn will be an invaluable aid to your understanding.

There is an excellent general Old Testament timeline in *Halley's Bible Handbook*.[3] Beginning with the approximate time of Adam's creation, major Biblical events such as the flood, the exodus of God's people from Egypt, the division of the kingdom into north and south, the captivity of Israel by the Babylonians, the destruction of Jerusalem, and the various efforts to rebuild Jerusalem and her walls are laid out with their approximate dates of happening. Distributed in correct chronological order among these events are the major characters that populate Old Testament history. It is wise to memorize the points of such a timeline because

---

3   Halley, Henry H., *Halley's Bible Handbook* (1965), p. 34, Zondervan Publishing
    House, Grand Rapids, Michigan.

it will give you a context into which all the other Biblically historical things you study can be inserted. You will be amazed how having such a timeline committed to memory will enhance all of your Biblical studies.

Chronology of Books and Events

The arrangement of books in the typical English translation of the Bible is not the chronological order in which they were written. Consequently, neither are the events they report. That is not a major deterrent to getting a correct handle on the message God gave us; however, part of considering the books in their historical setting may be realizing which were written earlier and which later. For example, relating Paul's letters to the historical timeline of events recorded in Acts provides a valuable perspective of Paul's work. The chart below shows Paul's activities in what is believed

Chronology of Paul's Journeys and Writings[4]

AD		
46 - 49	First Journey: Seleucia, Salamis, Paphos, Antioch in Pisidia, Iconium, Lystra and Derbe. On return, Paul preached in Perga and then on to Antioch.	
51 - 52	Second Journey: From Antioch with Silas through Cilicia, Lycaonia, and Galatia to Troas. Then to Philippi, Thessalonica, Berea, Athens, and Corinth.	
52 – 53	Living in Corinth	Wrote 1 Thessalonians, then 2 Thessalonians
Early 54	Left Corinth for Jerusalem and then on to Antioch	
Late 54	Third Journey: To Ephesus	
Early 57	In Ephesus	Wrote 1 Corinthians

4   Hall, Sewell, *New Testament Survey*, p. 81-83, Material is taken from Conybeare & Howson, *Life and Epistles of St. Paul*, (1963), William B. Eerdmans Publishing Co., Grand Rapids, Michigan, slightly amended in spots from J.W. McGarvey's commentary on *Acts of Apostles* (1872), Transylvania Printing and Publishing Co., Lexington, KY, now available in its entirety free online at www.ccel.org/m/mcgarvey/oca/OCA00A.HTM and www.studylight. org/com/oca.

Late 57	Travel to Macedonia	Wrote 2 Corinthians
57 – 58	In Corinth	Wrote Galatians and Romans
58	Left for Jerusalem, through Philippi and Miletus	
Mid 58	Arrested in Rome and sent to Caesarea	
60 - 61	Journey to Rome for trial	
62	In Rome	Wrote Philemon, Colossians, Ephesians and Philippians
66	Returned to Asia Minor	
Early 67	In Macedonia	Wrote 1 Timothy. If Paul wrote Hebrews, it was here.
Late 67	In Ephesus	Wrote Titus
68	In prison in Rome	Wrote 2 Timothy

to be their correct chronological order. If you were to follow Paul in a study of the book of Acts, you would necessarily encounter each of his letters along the way, the study of which would open Acts to you in a new and very special way.

The books in today's typical Bible are arranged in groups according to type of writing. The Old Testament starts with five books of law followed by books of history, poetry, and major and minor prophets. If the text were rearranged chronologically, Job would come before the middle of Genesis, David's psalms would be distributed throughout Kings and Chronicles that record his life, and many other changes would drastically reorder the present arrangement of books and verses.

There are several so-called chronological Bibles on the market, which in one way or another arrange the books of the Bible in the order of their writing. Any book that attempts to harmonize the gospels is a type of chronological Bible. William Arnold Steven's *A Harmony of the Gospels*,[5] which has been widely used for several decades, is this kind of book.

---

5   Stevens, William Arnold, *A Harmony of the Gospels* (1932), the 3rd edition published by Charles Scribner's Sons, New York.

If you are interested in a comprehensive rearrangement of Bible books, try F. LaGard Smith's *The Narrated Bible in Chronological Order*. It has been well received as evidenced by the fact it has been reprinted many times. One particularly intriguing feature is his treatment of the life of Jesus Christ. Another Bible student, Sam Dawson, has this to say of Smith's work: "In every event of Christ's life, he used a main text, perhaps a story in Matthew, which serves as the basis for a paragraph. Then that paragraph included a phrase, maybe from Luke, or maybe a word that only occurs in John. In this way, he weaved in all of the words and phrases from all of the gospels."[6]

A chronological Bible or two may prove to be a valuable addition to your library. They can be very effective aids to your understanding of Scripture.

Chapter 11 Discussion

1. How would you define the *overall* context of the Bible?

2. Explain the "funnel approach" to learning.

---

6 Dawson, Samuel G., *How to Study the Bible* (2005), pgs. 177–178, Gospel Themes Press, Amarillo, Texas.

3. Please indicate for each following whether TRUE or FALSE:

a. Today's meaning of the word "context" is to stitch together loosely. _____

b. Understanding the context is vital to a correct understanding of any part of the whole. _____

c. A complete and balanced understanding of any Biblical truth is possible only if it fits accurately within the overall context of the Bible. _____

d. If we know the dictionary meaning of a word, we will certainly understand the writer's use of it. _____

e. The "funnel approach" to learning involves pouring knowledge into the student's head. _____

f. An historical timeline explains the order in which things happened. _____

g. We have the books of the New Testament in the order in which they were written. _____

h. The true meaning of words can usually be determined by considering only the sentence in which they are used. _____

i. Rather than chronologically, books of the Bible are arranged by type of writing – law, history, poetry, prophecy, biography, etc. _____

j. Because Paul was not married he wrote, "It is good for a man not to touch a woman," meaning men and women should have no contact. _____

k. The book of Job was written after 2 Kings. _____

Chapter 11 Discussion

Biblical Authority

Who has the right to tell me what to do?

You mean not everyone is entitled to his or her own truth?

The two chapters following this deal with preparing to understand the Bible and the required steps for arriving at a correct understanding. With what attitude must we prepare, and how will we handle its message when obtained? Fundamental to any approach to Scripture is a healthy appreciation for its authority, the subject of this chapter. Though there is general agreement that the Bible is the Word of God, the broad community of Christianity is woefully and hopelessly divided on what its content means and how to apply it. Why? It is this writer's view that most differences in understanding and application derive from differing attitudes toward the authority of sacred Scriptures.

The Nature of Authority

Authority is universal. It is a part of one's life from birth throughout whatever endeavors lie ahead. The authority of parents, the schoolhouse, the community and business are a few obvious areas. Many of us embrace some "discipline" for livelihood and fulfilling achievement. It is called a discipline because of the rules and regulations it imposes upon us. A mathematician or computer programmer understands full well that success is possible only by careful observance of precise, rigid rules. A surgeon follows very strict procedures. Only meticulous adherence to the rules of the discipline will produce desired results.

Authority in human relationships involves submission of one person to another based upon a communicated standard of conduct or operation. There are two types: *inherent authority* (having the right to rule) and *delegated authority* (the right to rule in a limited realm as defined and authorized by the one with superior authority). The nature of delegated authority was described by Paul to those at Corinth: "But I want you to know that the head of every man is Christ, the head of woman is man, and the head of Christ is God." (1 Corinthians 11:3)

For what purpose does anyone use the Bible? Some may use it for purely literary reasons, but hopefully the vast majority uses it to learn about God's Savior and how we should live and worship to obtain His promise of eternal salvation. The inspired writer said, "And whatever you do in word or deed, do all in the name of the Lord Jesus,..." (Colossians 3:17) Saying or doing something in Christ's name means saying or doing it by His authority. If He did not authorize it, His disciples have no business engaging in it.

In this chapter, we will explore the nature of Biblical authority so that we might speak and do only as He has authorized.

Popular Views of Biblical Authority

Perhaps, before looking more carefully at Biblical authority, it would be beneficial to consider some of the diverse views held by those who claim to be Christians. You might be surprised at the far out views I have encountered. For example, a woman with whom I studied in a small village near the Polish town of Wadovice, claimed to be a devout Christian, vehemently supported Pope John Paul II (who was born in Wadovice), but disavowed belief in God! Need I say more about her view of the Bible as God's Word? Admittedly, this extreme is isolated, but rejection of Biblical authority within the ranks of Christianity is widespread. Of course, the Catholic Church, of which she is a member, has long held their traditions to be more authoritative than the Bible.

But it is not just Catholicism. Among certain denominations some are classifying fundamentalists as "Bible-believers" and distinguishing them from those with a more liberal view. Eddie Ekmekji, campus minister of the Inter Varsity Christian Fellowship at California State University, says of this persuasion, "Bible-believing is an awkward term. Ask two pastors of different denominations, and they may have their own criteria of what it means to identify someone or a church as a Bible-believer. One website mentioned that all Christians are Bible-believers because the scriptures inform our worldview. However, I can safely say that there are many people who consider themselves Christian (by culture and even by faith) but do not hold to the authority of scripture."[1]

Arguably, one of the most telling evidences that many professing to be Christians are running roughshod over the authority of Scripture came on July 7, 2002, when Jonathan Petre, Religion Correspondent for London's Daily Telegraph, filed this report of a newly released survey: "A third of Church of England clergy doubt or disbelieve in the physical Resurrection and only half are convinced of the truth of the Virgin birth, according to a new survey. The poll of nearly 2,000 of the Church's 10,000 clergy also found that only half believe that faith in Christ is the only route to salvation."[2]

---

1 Eddie Ekmekji, *Are you a Bible Believing Christian?* (2006), InterVarsity Christian Fellowship at California State University, Northridge, CA. See http://servingbread.net/2006/10/18/are-you-a-Bible-believing-christian/

2 Wright, N.T., *The Resurrection of the Son of God (Christian Origins and the Question of God)* (First North American edition: 2003), in the *Introduction* , Augsburg Fortress, Publishers, Minneapolis, MN, citing *One Third Of Anglican Clergy Do Not Believe In The Resurrection*, Daily Telegraph (London, England) article filed July 31, 2002, by Religion Correspondent Jonathan Petre.

This view of the broad community of Christianity is shocking to many, but the more important issue is where you and I stand regarding Biblical authority. Following are a number of views of the Bible, most of which have been expressed by those who profess to be Christians. Is your view represented in this list?

"It doesn't make any difference how you worship as long as you are expressing love for God."

"There are many ways to God: Buddhism, Hinduism, Judaism, Islam, Christianity. Any way is okay."

"I did it because God spoke directly to my heart."

"If I didn't do it this way, I would be dishonoring my mother who always did it this way."

"Jesus promised that the Holy Spirit would guide me into all truth, so I am comfortable in the knowledge that what I understand is from the Spirit."

"The Bible is a good book written by men; while it has many good moral lessons, it is largely mythical and is not to be believed as truth."

"As long as you live a good moral life and generally do good deeds toward your neighbor, God will be pleased with you."

"As long as we are sincere, it makes no difference how we worship."

"The Bible is God's Word, but it is corrupted. Our religious leader has received from God a latter day revelation which more accurately reveals God's message for us today."

"We've always done it this way, and our fathers before us."

"This is the way our church has taught it."

"Let's not change it; it works well this way."

"It does good; therefore, it must be right."

"Other religious groups or churches are doing it."

"God is not that strict; He is a loving God who doesn't get hung up on details of how we believe or behave or worship."

"We Are All One. Ours is not a better way, ours is merely another way."[3]

"But how can we know for sure what is Divine Inspiration and what is not? How can we be certain who is speaking eternal truth? ... We do not have to know. All we have to know is *our* truth, not someone else's."[4]

Though these views are often voiced, not one can be supported with Holy Writ. The last two comments are naked New Age, but as a group they smack of religious humanism, a belief-system in which the individual sits as judge over truth and determines what constitutes the divine will. Sadly, most of these beliefs are often espoused by those who wear the name Christian.

In responding to these views as a group, a number of Bible passages come to mind. First, Paul insisted that proper knowledge is necessary to back our actions. There are those, Paul said, that "have a zeal for God, but not according to knowledge." (Romans 10:2) Why, Paul? "For they being ignorant of God's righteousness, and seeking to establish their own righteousness, have not submitted to the righteousness of God." (Romans 10:3)

How successfully might we expect man to establish his own righteousness, his own religion? Solomon made a wise observation, which he immediately followed with a logical question: "A man's steps are of the Lord. How then can a man understand his own way?" (Proverbs 20:24) The prophet Jeremiah provided answer when he admitted to the Lord: "O Lord, I know the way of man is not in himself; It is not in man who walks to direct his own steps." (Jeremiah 10:23) God also answers this question: "For as the heavens are higher than the earth, So are My ways higher than your ways, And My thoughts than your thoughts." (Isaiah 55:9)

Even though their efforts are wrapped in religious, even Christian trappings, those who try to establish their own way are foolish.

3 Walsch, Neale Donald, *The New Revelation, A Conversation with God* (2004), p. 210, Atria Books, New Your, NY.

4 Walsch, Neale Donald, *Communion with God* (2000), p. 3, G. P. Putnam's Sons, New Youk, NY.

The Supremacy of God

It is not hard to find expressions of authority in Nature. Many natural laws are absolute and unbending, and predictably so. They extend no mercy. If you defy the law of gravity or human tolerance for heat or cold, you will likely pay. Fly in the face of Nature's authority, and you will likely pay a heavy price, perhaps your life. The society at large, even those who do not believe in God or claim to follow Jesus, bow in respect for Nature's authority.

The fact is, God is a higher authority than Nature. He created the universe and all that is in it. If we so carefully mold our lives to Nature's demands, why not to the One who made and controls Nature? Isn't it odd that throughout history men have easily elevated their thoughts and traditions above God's commands, and though Jesus Christ clearly condemned it, men professing to be His followers continue to do it today? Christ's condemnation of the Pharisees is easily understood: "Hypocrites! Well did Isaiah prophecy about you, saying, 'These people draw near to Me with their mouth, And honor Me with their lips, But their heart is far from Me. And in vain do they worship Me, Teaching as doctrines the commandments of men.'" (Matthew 15:7-9)

Still, some unashamedly hold to their traditions above God's will as He revealed it in the Bible, and find rationale for doing so. The Catholic Church elevates its traditions above the Bible, and claims their traditions are not the same kind as those of men that Jesus condemned. They claim a difference in their traditions: they are inspired. In his essay *What is the Relationship Between Scripture and Tradition?*, Mark Shea defends the Catholic position by arguing that many inspired traditions from God have been passed down outside of the written Word.[5] A Catholic priest once explained to me that the Bible is only part of God's truth for mankind, the

---

5 Shea, Mark P., *Essay: What is the Relationship Between Scripture and Tradition?* From *Not By Scripture Alone: A Catholic Critique of the Protestant Doctrine of Sola Scriptura* (1997), Robert Sungenis, ed., Queenship, Santa Barbara, CA.

The Supremacy of God

rest being those "truths" (such as the doctrine of the assumption of Mary) that came to Catholic minds, thoughts which survived the test of time.

Did God reveal additional truth for our guidance by the channel of Catholic Church traditions? Similarly, did He reveal a latter day gospel for North America to Joseph Smith as is claimed by the Mormon Church? If God has added to His first century revelation to New Testament writers by traditions or latter day revelations, He has contradicted clear claims He made in the Bible:

o When Jude wrote late in the first century, he understood that "the faith… was *once for all (italicized emphasis mine, CB)* delivered to the saints." (vs. 3) The delivered faith was "once for all" as was the sacrifice of our Lord. (Hebrews 10:10) If we need more revelations today, we need additional crucifixions and resurrections. Was Jude's message inspired? Did God say in the first century that the body of faith was already delivered, or did He say it would continue to come to various individuals throughout the following centuries?

o After affirming that all Scripture was given by inspiration, Paul wrote of its purpose, "…that the man of God may be complete, thoroughly equipped for every good work." (2 Timothy 3:17) Were early disciples who had all of the New Testament writings "thoroughly equipped for every good work?" Which of the later allegedly inspired traditions of the Catholic Church did they need in order to be perfected in Christ? What teaching that Joseph Smith espoused in the 19th century was needed by those who went before?

Could it be that some throughout history have considered what the Bible teaches and decided it isn't to their liking or that they can improve upon God's message? It is not within man to direct his own steps. If the source of authority in religion is not divine, it must be human, and therefore, inferior.

God's Revelation to Mankind

God created mankind for a purpose – His purpose. Having crafted a creature with the ability to reason and make choices, He obligated Himself to provide a standard of right. Having molded a being for the purpose of loving Him, He was obligated to reveal Himself and His will for humanity. He used two ways – *general revelation* and *special revelation* – to accomplish this.

General Revelation

The psalmist David opened his beautiful 19th Psalm with a proclamation of the Lord's general revelation about Himself: "The heavens declare the glory of God; And the firmament shows His handiwork." (vs. 1) God's general revelation of Himself to mankind is continuous. It makes no difference when or where one lives, or what language he or she speaks, one needs only look up or all around at the physical universe to know that God exists.

The fact that we were created "in the image of God" (Genesis 1:27) is further evidence of God's existence. He gave us the ability to reason, deduce and form decisions. He made each of us with the ability to weigh evidence and either accept it in belief or reject it in disbelief. He formed all living things on the basis of design, often intricate design, and instilled us with the understanding that all intelligent design requires an intelligent designer. His general revelation is sufficiently forceful to cause us to believe there is a God.

Since His general revelation is spread out before everyone with mental capacity, without exception, we are all called upon to decide. Paul spoke of those who would reject the evidence, those whom he said "...suppress the truth in unrighteousness because what may be known of God is manifest in them, for God has shown it to them. For since the creation of the world His invisible attributes are clearly seen, being understood by the things that are made, even His eternal power and Godhead, so that they are without excuse, because, although they knew God, they did not glorify Him as God, nor were thankful, but became futile in their thoughts, and their foolish hearts were darkened." (Romans 1:18-21) We dare not allow ourselves to be counted among that number.

Special Revelation

The special revelation of God is the written Word of God we have in the sixty-six books of the Bible. God created us for the purpose of loving and trusting in Him, growing in His image day by day. We can see God's power, intelligence and creativity in the physical universe, but we could not know of His love and mercy and His special purpose for us without His written Word. Just as he wrote of God's general revelation, David spoke of God's special revelation in the second stanza of the 19ᵗʰ Psalm: "The law of the Lord is perfect, converting the soul; The testimony of the Lord is sure, making wise the simple; The statutes of the Lord are right, rejoicing the heart; The commandment of the Lord is pure, enlightening the eyes; The fear of the Lord is clean, enduring forever; The judgments of the Lord are true and righteous altogether. More to be desired are they than gold, Yea, than much fine gold; Sweeter also than honey and the honeycomb. Moreover by them Your servant is warned, And in keeping them there is great reward." (vss. 7-11) While general revelation leaves us wanting to know more about God's nature and what He wants of us, delving into His special revelation makes it clear.

Inspiration

Paul told Timothy, "All scripture is given by inspiration of God,…" (2 Timothy 3:16) The word *inspiration* (*theopneustos* in Greek) means "inspired by God" (*Theos*, "God," *pneō*, "to breathe").[6] What God breathed were words, an infallible message

---

6   Vine, W.E., *Vine's Expository Dictionary of New Testament Words* (1984), p. 328, Thomas Nelson Publishers, Nashville, Tennessee.

in the language of fallible man. God, who is timeless, spoke pure, divine words of truth in the faulty language of historical man. Why? Clearly, it is because any effective communication must be presented in terms the intended hearers can understand.

Of the process, Peter wrote, "...holy men of God spoke as they were moved by the Holy Spirit." (2 Peter 1:21) Paul amplified Peter's explanation: "But as it is written: 'Eye has not seen, nor ear heard, Nor have entered into the heart of man The things which God has prepared for those who love Him.' But God has revealed them to us through His Spirit. For the Spirit searches all things, yes, the deep things of God.... Now we have received not the spirit of the world, but the Spirit who is from God, that we might know the things that have been freely given to us by God. These things also we speak, not in words which man's wisdom teaches but which the Holy Spirit teaches, comparing spiritual things with spiritual." (1 Corinthians 2:9-13) There is no room for later revelation in the process the apostles described.

Both apostles spoke of the Spirit's involvement in the process. The Spirit searched *all* things of God, things He had prepared for those who love Him. Did the Spirit miss something, or did He fail to pass on what He learned? No. The Spirit revealed all of God's will necessary to our salvation, all that God wants us to know. There is no room for nor need of afterthoughts.

Jesus spoke with divine authority (Matthew 24:35; John 6:63), and Peter considered the letters of Paul to be Scripture. (2 Peter 3:14-16) The early church quoted the New Testament in the same manner as the Old, treating all these writings as God-given words.[7]

The New Testament affirms inspiration of the Old Testament, including its prophecies of the coming Messiah. (John 5:46; Luke 24:44; Acts 10:43) According to His use of Scripture, there is no

---

7   Marshall, Howard, *Biblical Inspiration* (1982), pgs. 19-30, Eerdmans, Grand Rapids, Michigan.

doubt that Jesus believed the Old Testament contained the inspired Words of God. (Matt. 5:18; Mark 12:35-37; John 10:34-36)

God used the instrumentality of men to convey His message. He gave them each the words that they wrote without overriding the individual styles with which they wrote. The prophets and apostles never took personal credit for their messages, but prefaced their message with "Thus saith the Lord."

Before leaving this discussion of divine inspiration, it should be noted that all of the evidence we have insists Biblical inspiration is both *verbal* (with words) and *plenary* (complete in every respect).

The Inerrancy of Scripture

God's Word is truth (John 17:17); it can be trusted because it is inerrant, that is, *free from error*, or infallible. *Infallibility* means *incapaple of error, unerring*.[8] Of course, we would not expect an infallible God to give a fallible message. Since God cannot lie (Titus 1:2; Hebrews 6:17, 18), and the Bible is divinely inspired, it must be true and completely trustworthy in its entirety – as it claims to be. Inerrancy is the result of inspiration.

Not only was the Bible infallible when written, it remains generally so today. God has protected its transmission through ensuing generations right down to the present time. Any slight differences in manuscript copies during the transmission process are insignificant to the overall message, and the few errors found in some translations are equally innocuous. For example, 2 Kings 2:23 in the King James translation should read "young men," not "little children." And Acts 12:4 has the inaccurate word "Easter" which should be "Passover." (Greek *pascha* is translated correctly as Passover in Matthew 26:2 and other places.) While the latter has been used to justify observance of Easter, as a group these errors do not materially alter the overall message. There are other similar

---

8   *Webster's Ninth New Collegiate Dictionary* (1985), p. 618, Merriam-Webster Inc., Springfield, Massachusetts.

translation errors, but none which have materially affected the inerrancy of God's Word.

Since His Word is inerrant, men have no right to tamper with it. Solomon affirmed this fact long ago: "Every word of God is pure; He is a shield to those who put their trust in Him. Do not add to His words, Lest He rebuke you, and you be found a liar." (Proverbs 30:5)

Handling Aright the Word of Truth

Every Bible student has a responsibility to "rightly divide" or "handle aright" the Word of truth. (2 Timothy 2:15) The fact that a supreme God with all authority gave us His inerrant message lays upon us the responsibility to carefully analyze it and diligently strive to understand it correctly. How to do that is the subject of this and the next two chapters. More generally, it is the purpose of this book.

Suffice to note here that handling aright starts with an attitude of respect for truth. We must love it. (2 Thessalonians 2:9, 10) You say you don't love study and never have? You will, if with a positive attitude, you invest yourself – your time and resources – in gaining the knowledge and developing the skills involved in effective study. Your respect and love for truth will grow in the process. Do you doubt it? Give it a try with the desire to love truth!

How the Bible Authorizes

The Bible nowhere offers a clear formula for determining what is authoritative for us today. Understanding what God expects is mostly common sense. Living according to God's instructions is not much different than following the directions in a chemistry book to achieve a certain chemical result, or adhering to instructions given for assembling a bicycle, or behaving according to the code of conduct laid down by a loving parent. It involves doing only what is stated to do, only what is authorized without taking personal license with the directions.

While repeating to the people all that God had said to him, Moses said, "Therefore you shall be careful to do as the Lord your God has commanded you; you shall not turn aside to the right hand or to the left. You shall walk in all the ways which the Lord your God has commanded you,..." (Deuteronomy 5:32, 33) How can we sift through all that is in the Bible – the reported words and deeds of ungodly men, God's exclusive instructions to others, historical notations, etc. – to find only that which applies to us? While there is no explicit formula for doing so, we can learn by considering how Scripture handles Scripture. The following tried and true, common sense guidelines will help us recognize the elements of Biblical authority.

Direct Statements

The Bible authorizes by direct statements. Often we hear this referred to as direct command, but direct statement seems to be a more accurate classification. Hugh Fulford points out that the terminology *direct command* is less inclusive than direct statement: "...direct command does not fully convey the way in which the Bible may authorize a matter. *Commands* are *imperative statements* which do indeed authorize, but there are other kinds of statements which give authority as well."[9] And so there are. Let's notice some as used by Bible writers.

First, please recognize that in the English language there are four kinds of statements, or sentences: declarative, interrogative, imperative and exclamatory. While we find authority more frequently in some than in others, it is advisable to consider each.

---

9 Fulford, Hugh, *Determining Bible Authority*, as presented in the *27th Annual Spiritual Sword Lectureship* at the Getwell Church of Christ, Memphis, Tennessee, published in *The Authority of the Bible* (2002), p. 202, Sain Publications, Pulaski, Tennessee.

Declarative statements – Declarations are common to our speech and generally have the purpose of stating, telling, or conveying some information – to make some truth known. If someone says, "Jesus is Lord," and someone else says, "Allah is Lord," both are statements purporting to be truth, but both cannot be true. The declarations are mutually exclusive. Christians know Jesus as God in flesh. Muslims deny that Allah ever became flesh and dwelled with humanity. Statements are either true or false according to the absolute standard of truth. There are many declarative statements in Scripture. Here are some, which authorize action on our part:

o Hosea closes his prophecy with these declarations: "For the ways of the Lord are right; the righteous walk in them, But transgressors stumble in them." (Hosea 14:9) Hosea points us to the right way where the righteous walk and warns against stumbling as the transgressors.

o In his declaration of why God brought us forth ("Of His own will He brought us forth by the Word of truth, that we might be a kind of firstfruits of His creatures." (James 1:18)), James gives us reason to conduct ourselves according to the divine purpose. This declaration, given in the New Covenant, authorizes our conduct today.

o The Hebrews writer stated: "For if we sin willfully after we have received the knowledge of the truth, there no longer re-mains a sacrifice for sins." (Hebrews 10:26) There is authority in this statement for at least two actions: refrain from willful sin (stated in the positive: always submit to God's will) and work to gain knowledge of the truth that we might recognize and avoid sin.

Interrogative statements – The term *interrogative statements* may seem a misstatement. We don't normally think of questions as state-ments. Still, interrogative sentences (or statements) fall into one of the four technical classifications of English statements. And, on occasion we find God's authority in an interrogative. They usually take the form of questions designed to seek or elicit information, or that of rhetorical questions, which are typically asked to make a point. Some examples will help:

o "The cup of blessing which we bless, is it not the communion of the blood of Christ? The bread which we break, is it not the communion of the body of Christ?" (1 Corinthians 10:16) Paul was not seeking information. The answer to both questions is obvious. He was simply emphasizing his point, and in doing so giving us authority for correct observance of the Lord's Supper.

o Jesus spoke to Martha, the sister of Lazarus whose body lay in the tomb, in three declarative statements followed by an interrogative: "I am the resurrection and the life. He who believes in Me, though he may die, he shall live. And whoever lives and believes in Me shall never die. Do you believe this?" (John 11:25, 26) Jesus asked Martha for information, or since He knows the heart, He asked to hear her confess her belief. This is an interrogative statement from which we learn that it is approved to believe in the declarations He made.

o "Now when they heard this, they were cut to the heart, and said to Peter and the rest of the apostles, 'Men and brethren, what shall we do?'" (Acts 2:37) Peter had preached to them Jesus, the resurrected One they had slain. Upon feeling the pangs of guilt for their sin, they cried out, "What shall we do?" Here is authority for a godly response when one is confronted with the realization of his or her own sins.

Not all interrogative sentences authorize actions we should take. Some do. Watch for them.

Imperative statements – Imperative statements are commands. In very direct and forceful language they tell us what or what not to do. Consider these important scriptural imperatives:

o The letter to the Romans is filled with imperative statements, commands to live righteously: "Render therefore to all their due: taxes to whom taxes are due, customs to whom customs,

Direct Statements

fear to whom fear, honor to whom honor." (13:7) "Owe no one anything except to love one another,…" (13:8) "But put on the Lord Jesus Christ, and make no provision for the flesh, to fulfill its lusts." (13:14)

o "Go therefore and make disciples of all the nations,…" (Matthew 28:19) This statement in English appears to include two imperative verbs: "go" and "make." However, there is some thought that "go" is not an imperative verb in Greek. Some later translations of the New Testament render the thought "as you are going" or "wherever you go." It is true, early disciples were already a going group. Perhaps they did not need to be told to go. Looking to the Greek, *poreuomai*, the meaning is "to go on one's way, to proceed from one place to another."[10] Whether or not "go" is an imperative verb, the statement Jesus made to them is imperative. Go and make disciples. It is a command, and as such, hard to mistake what the Lord wants of us. As we go on our way, wherever we go, we are obligated to make disciples for Him.

Exclamatory statements – Exclamatory statements may express excitement, surprise, disgust or annoyance. They may include authorization for some action for they might also be classed declarative or imperative statements with force.

o John the Baptist looked out and exclaimed, "Behold! The Lamb of God who takes away the sin of the world!" (John 1:29) John's declaration is rich with divine authority. Here is the One who takes away the sins of the world, a meek and innocent Lamb destined for sacrifice. He came on the highest authority, and by His very appearance He solicits our love and allegiance, our devotion and obedience.

o Jesus insisted with authority, "Take these things away! Do not make My Father's house a house of merchandise!" (John 2:16)

---

10 Vine, W.E., *Vine's Expository Dictionary of New Testament Words* (1984), p. 269, Thomas Nelson Publishers, Nashville, Tennessee.

Woe to those today who ignore the force of these commands and misuse those things He has set apart as sacred.

Approved Examples

Another important way the Bible authorizes is by *approved example*. We sometimes hear this referred to as *approved apostolic example*. Of course, if early disciples set the example and it is not corrected by an inspired apostle or some other clear teaching, it is fair to conclude that it is approved by God. But the real import of an approved example is that it is approved by God.

There are many examples in Scripture of ungodly behavior that should not be followed. For example, there is the man who had his father's wife and the church in Corinth was "puffed up" over the sexual immorality among them. (1 Corinthians 5:1, 2) Also, in the Old Testament, do you remember the case of King Saul who kept the spoils of battle in violation of God's command to destroy everything? (1 Samuel 15:3, 24) We must imitate only those examples with God's clear approval.

Someone may ask why? Why should we be concerned about approved examples? The answer is they give us valuable guidance by providing us a *pattern* of the practices and behaviors with which God is pleased. Some have insisted that there are no Biblical patterns to be followed, despite the fact that inspired writers were well aware of them.

o The author of Hebrews, discussing the priesthood of Christ, made a point of the fact that Moses was commanded to make the tabernacle according to the *pattern* he was shown on the mountain. (Hebrews 8:5; Exodus 25:40)

o Paul wrote the young evangelist Timothy: "...for this reason I obtained mercy, that in me first Jesus Christ might show all longsuffering, as a *pattern* to those who are going to believe on Him for eternal life." (1 Timothy 1:16)

o Old Testament writers also knew the importance of following the divine patterns which God gave from time to time
   throughout the history of His people. (Exodus 25:9; Numbers
   8:4 and 22:28; Ezekiel 43:10)

The same idea of a pattern to be followed is expressed in Scripture in other ways. Paul wrote the Roman church, "But God be
thanked that though you were slaves of sin, yet you obeyed from
the heart that form of doctrine to which you were delivered."
(Romans 6:17) There is a form, a pattern of doctrinal matters giv-
en by God. Our task is to discern it and pattern our lives after it.

When you locate an approved example, it is wise to recognize
that not all are equal. There are *restrictive examples* and *non-restrictive examples*. Let's notice the difference in a few approved Biblical
examples.

Non-restrictive examples – A non-restrictive example is one that
authorizes one to act in the same way, but does not require it
because either that example or others broaden the authority to
include similar actions. In other words, it is permissive but not
restrictive.

o When Paul raised the question, "Do we have no right to take
   along a believing wife,…" (1 Corinthians 9:5) he used the example of the other apostles, the Lord's brothers and Peter
   to show that he had the authority to marry as well. Their example gave him the right to marry, but did not require it. He
   never did. The example was permissive but not restrictive.

o Dorcas made tunics and garments. (Acts 9:39) This example
   authorizes but does not bind anyone to do what she did.
   Why? Other widows standing by on that occasion, apparently
   approved by the apostle Peter, showed Dorcas' garments but
   did not make them.

o Lydia and her friends had a custom of meeting at the riverside for prayer, and Paul explained salvation to them there.
   (Acts 16:11-15) Their encounter authorizes us to meet at a

riverside for prayer, and it provides authority for us to preach to lost souls at such a place. Does it require us to do that? No. Many other Scriptural examples show that folks prayed in a variety of places and preached wherever they found those who might listen, thus broadening the authority to other venues.

Restrictive examples – A restrictive example is one which stands alone as the only authority for the action, or its details preclude any other similar action.

○ The Lord instructed us to remember His death by partaking of the Lord's Supper, but did not say when or how often to do it. Lacking any apostolic instruction, we look for a New Testament example of the time and frequency with which early Christians observed the supper, and find it in Acts 20. Paul and his company sailed from Philippi to Troas where they waited seven days to meet with the saints on the first day of the week to eat the Lord's Supper. (Acts 20:6, 7) (It should be noted that Jewish reckoning of time counted partial days as whole ones. Waiting seven days until Sunday means they arrived on Monday after the supper had been eaten for that week.) Why didn't Paul convince them to eat the supper earlier, say on Tuesday or Wednesday, so he could continue on his journey? Lacking any other evidence we must conclude that meeting on Sunday, the first day of the week, was the approved time to partake of the supper. We find no other example to authorize a different day. To observe the Lord's Supper on any other day but Sunday is to do so on human authority, not God's.

○ In the first century, the leadership of every fully organized church was a plurality of qualified elders. After completing his first missionary journey, Paul returned and "appointed elders in every church." (Acts 14:23) Later when in Miletus, Paul "sent to Ephesus and called for the elders of the church" (Acts 20:17) to meet with him. Paul addressed his letter to the

Approved Examples

Philippian church: "To all the saints who are in Christ Jesus who are in Philippi, with the bishops (a term synonymous with "elders" in New Testament times) and deacons." (Philippians 1:1) And in his letter to Titus, the evangelist, Paul said, "appoint elders in every city, as I commanded you." (Titus 1:5) Every mention of elders in the early church is in the plural form. There is no example at all of a single elder, or a single bishop for that matter, in a position of leadership in the Lord's church. Our conclusion: if a church appoints elders as its leaders, there must be at least two. Further, they must be men who meet the qualifications that Paul, by inspiration of the Holy Spirit, wrote to Timothy and Titus. (1 Timothy 3:1-7; Titus 1:6-9) No others will do. There is no authority for a single man or a man without believing children or a woman to serve in that capacity. The examples we have coupled with the instructions given about whom to appoint, restrict us to choosing a plurality of men qualified by the Holy Spirit.

Remember this imperative statement: "…whatever you do in word or deed, do all in the name of (by the authority of – *insertion mine, CB*) the Lord Jesus,…" (Colossians 3:17)

Necessary Inference

The Bible authorizes by necessary inference. A necessary inference is a necessary conclusion, an implied conclusion that cannot be escaped though no such conclusion is explicitly stated in the text. Please take note that not all inferences are necessary. A student who loves truth and who is truly submitted to God's Word will carefully dismiss all possible conclusions that are not necessary to the passage.

o To demonstrate how necessary inference or conclusion works, let's go back to our earlier discussion regarding the Lord's Supper. About the meeting of Paul with Christians at Troas, the text says, "Now on the first day of the week, when the disciples came together to break bread,..." (Acts 20:7) The language does not tell us how often they met. Was it only that one time or more often? Meeting to partake of the supper only once does not fit the command of Jesus which authorized the observance. He said, "This do, as often as you drink it, in remembrance of Me." (1 Corinthians 11:25) So there must be a frequency with which they partook. What conclusion can be drawn from the language? The language "on the first day of the week" does not fit meeting once monthly. If it did, the day of the month would be given. By the same reasoning, it does not fit a quarterly meeting. Some have supposed yearly maybe because the Lord's Supper was instituted during the Passover Feast, an annual celebration. But that is no help since we are obligated to seek authority for how to do it in the New Covenant, not in the Old. The command to remember Him is similar to Jehovah's command in the Old Law: "Remember the Sabbath day, to keep it holy." (Exodus 20:8) God's people had no problem understanding that they were to keep *every* Sabbath day holy. Considering all of this, there is only one necessary conclusion that fits the example of Christians in Troas eating the Lord's Supper in the first century. They did it on the first day of *every* week.

o   When Saul, later referred to as the apostle Paul, recounted the events of his conversion, he told of being blind three days before God sent help. He said, "Ananias... came to me; and he stood and said to me, 'Brother Saul, receive your sight.' And at the same hour I looked up to him. Then he said, ...And now why are you waiting? Arise, and be baptized, and wash away your sins, calling on the name of the Lord." (Acts 22:12-16) The following are all necessary inferences from the command given Saul by Ananias:

1.   Paul was in a sinful state until after he was baptized.

2.   His baptism was total immersion in water for that was the only meaning of the act in the first century.

Necessary Inference

3. His sins were washed away, remitted by God during his immersion in water.

4. Calling on the name of the Lord is accomplished by obeying the Lord's command to be baptized.

That's a lot of inference, you say? You're right, and Ananias did not explicitly say any of this. Still, what Ananias did say infers these conclusions, and we can find no contradiction of any in other passages. Nor can we find any other form or reason for water baptism under the New Covenant. Other Scriptures support these conclusions. (Romans 6:3-6 and 10:13; Mark 16:16; Acts 8:36-38) Consequently, we conclude that honesty demands we consider these conclusions inescapable.

Necessary inference is an essential element in determining all that the Lord wants us to do and teach. Every well equipped Bible student will cultivate the skill to deal correctly with the implications of Scripture.

Expediency

The Bible authorizes by expediency. An expedient is anything that assists or expedites the authorized action. Any action, whether authorized for us today or not, may have expedients, but the only authorized expedients are those which expedite an authorized action. It can be anything that is beneficial to or helps achieve the authorized end, provided the expedient itself is not sinful. Notice a couple of New Testament passages which include the thought of expediency, or advantage:

o The Jewish high priest advised that the death of Jesus would be expedient for the Jewish people, suggesting that Christ's death would strengthen the nation's position with the Romans who dominated them. (John 18:14)

o Paul wrote to the Corinthians, "It is to your advantage not only to be doing what you began and were desiring to do a year ago; but now you also must complete the doing of it;…" (2 Corinthians 8:10, 11)

Expediency is also important for modern disciples of our Lord as we seek His authority for what we do. In fact, expediency is involved in the authority we have for most things we do. Consider the following:

○ A place to assemble is an expedient for the command of the Hebrews writer to "…consider one another in order to stir up love and good works, not forsaking the assembling of ourselves together,…" (Hebrews 10:24, 25) We could not meet for worship and mutual edification if we had no place to meet. Since meeting together is authorized, the expediencies of acquiring and maintaining a place to meet are authorized. Are stealing or murdering authorized expedients for acquiring a place? No, they would be sinful, but any righteous expedient would be authorized.

○ Cups for the fruit of the vine as well as trays to hold the cups and the bread are necessary expedients allowing us to carry out the Lord's instructions to remember His death.

○ Song books and pitch pipes are expedients which enable us to sing as Paul commanded. (Musical instruments are not expedients. They are a different kind of music from singing, a kind for which we have no New Covenant authority.)

○ A baptistery and baptismal garments are expedients that assist us in carrying out the Lord's command to baptize lost souls into the death of Christ that they might be cleansed by His blood and arise to a new life in Him. (Romans 6:3-8; Gal. 3:27)

There is no doubt that expedients are an important part of our authority for worshipping and serving in Christ. Before closing this discussion of expedients, please understand there is no authority in expedients apart from an authoritative direct statement or approved example, which they expedite.

Expediency

165

Cultural Considerations

This may be the most difficult area of Biblical authority on which to get a handle. As I begin writing this section, I am keenly aware of my responsibility and my lack of clear understanding of this subject. I have sought the Lord's help in prayer, and have proceeded with writing in the hope my feeble thoughts will help you decide how to understand cultural customs in the early church.

It is becoming more and more common to hear of women entering the pulpits and positions of leadership in a number of denominations of Christianity. They do this despite prohibitions in Scripture against women taking positions of leadership. The argument being used to set aside Scriptural prohibitions is that such prohibitions pertain only to the culture in which they were given. "They are not timeless truth," it is said. Is there anything substantive to this argument? Are there some matters in Scripture that should be understood in light of cultural custom, matters that do not apply in a culture that the practice does not fit?

There are, in fact, some practices in New Testament times that churches in America have generally not adopted. Is it because they are foreign to our culture? Jesus washed the apostles' feet telling them to do the same, the apostles commanded early Christians to greet one another with a holy kiss, and the culture as well as the apostles forbade women to speak in the assembly and occupy any leadership role. How should we handle these commands today? Are they timeless truth that must be obeyed? Or are they simply a part of that early culture, which we need not adopt?

It would seem that Paul accommodated himself to culture when he told slaves to obey their masters without condemning the practice of slavery. (Ephesians 6:5) Is slavery okay with God? Because of various Biblical principles – love for all men, counting the other person better than self, all are made in the image of God, etc. – we probably would conclude it is not. Did Paul not deal with slavery believing that in time the principles he taught would overcome and change the culture? If so, it opens the door for us to condone, even practice, ungodliness because it is cultural, as long as we can hope that in time our teaching will overcome and change the culture. Did the apostles and early disciples have their hands full establishing churches and carrying the gospel to the world without tackling the political and economic issues involved with slavery? Not including slavery in our evangelistic strategy may seem a sensible plan for men, but perhaps the Lord had other reasons for not directing the apostles to teach directly against slavery. We do not know. Until we do, the New Testament's treatment of first century slavery does not appear to help us find a solution for dealing with cultural customs. Still, we can safely conclude from the many passages that enjoin love and respect for others, it would be wrong for us to enslave our neighbor.

So, the question is, how can we determine when a Biblical statement or example is merely a cultural custom that is not to be literally practiced in our culture? Let's try to determine how to handle what appear to be obvious cases of scriptural authority wrapped in cultural settings. As we do, we will be analyzing for the purpose of answering certain questions.

Questions to Answer

When analyzing what appear to be cultural practices, we are trying to determine —

1. Does the practice and its particular details have universal application *or* is it limited in its scope and application to the time and place in which we find it?

2. Can it be applied to all people of all places and ages?

3. How do other passages harmonize or shed light on the "cultural practice?" Do they indicate that the practice itself should be bound upon all universally, or is the practice setting forth simply a universal principle to be obeyed?

Cultural Considerations

As indicated earlier, answering these questions correctly may not be easy. The evidence we weigh in reaching answers must be the inspired Word of God, not human wisdom about which cultural practices fit or seem universal, and which do not.

Foot Washing

During the first century much of travel was by sandal clad feet, which became dirty from the dusty roadways. Feet were washed often, and a host normally provided a wash basin with water for his guests. If there were servants, they washed the guests' feet, and the task was considered to be the most demeaning they were called upon to do. So, foot washing was not only a necessity due to travel conditions at that time, but also a sign of hospitality humbly given. When Jesus washed the apostles' feet, He was demonstrating with a common act of humble service the lesson He wanted to teach. He was showing them hospitality in the most demeaning way. After washing all of their feet and reseating Himself, Jesus explained to the apostles what He had done. I believe there is real significance in what Jesus said. Let's notice all of the passage, and then analyze His words: "Do you know what I have done to you? You call me Teacher and Lord, and you say well, for so I am. If I then, your Lord and Teacher, have washed your feet, you also ought to wash one another's feet. For I have given you an example, that you should do as I have done to you. Most assuredly, I say to you, a servant is not greater than his master; nor is he who is sent greater than he who sent him." (John 13:12-16)

My view: It seems obvious that the Lord's primary lesson was service one to the other. He reminded them of His superiority, and had them understand that even He, their Lord and Teacher, was not too important to serve them in a very demeaning way. He summarized His explanation with the statement, "...a servant is not greater than his master; nor is he who is sent greater than he who sent him." When Jesus said, "For I have given you an example, that you should do as I have done to you," He was not telling us to wash feet, but rather to serve one another even if we are demeaned by the doing. This is the timeless lesson to be learned and practiced. He used the most demeaning form of hospitality their culture offered to demonstrate the lesson. We should be willing to do no less. If living in a culture today where foot washing was a common necessity or a means of showing hospitality, we would be obligated to happily take up our towel and basin and begin washing.

The Holy Kiss

Paul encouraged Roman Christians to "Greet one another with a holy kiss." (16:16) Peter similarly instructed a larger audience of disciples to "Greet one another with a kiss of love." (1 Peter 5:14) There are many cultures in our modern world that find this practice familiar and embrace it easily. Years ago, while visiting a church in Paris, France, I witnessed arriving members greeting one another with a kiss on the cheek. To them it was natural, even among unbelievers. It is interesting, though, that they modified the practice from what I expect was practiced in New Testament times. Adults of opposite gender did not kiss one another unless the one kissed was elderly. Only children and the very old greeted me with a kiss. I suppose their restraint was part of their culture for propriety's sake.

People in America, even in the church, are not as comfortable with the practice of greeting with a kiss. We generally encourage observing the principle without literal obedience to the command. Is that correct interpretation? Does this command embody a principle to be observed or is the practice a timeless truth to be obeyed literally? To this Bible student, the former seems the case. The kiss is a cultural custom to which we are not bound. The principle of giving one another a holy and loving greeting is the practice to which we are bound.

Women as Preachers and Elders

The leaders at the highest levels of various denominations have set about to resolve the question of women in leadership roles. The introduction to one such effort bears this statement: "There are many doctrines that are essential to Christian faith—for example, the church must teach that there is only one God, and that we are saved by grace through faith in Jesus Christ. Yet there are many other doctrines that are not essential to our faith, but are practical guidelines or policies for our physical life, and these may differ from culture to culture, or from one time in history to another. We *want* to get them right, but we must also understand they are not essential to what it means to be a Christian. We believe that eldership of women is one of those doctrines. It is a policy matter, not part of the *Statement of Beliefs*. People do not need to leave the church if they think we are wrong about the millennium, nor do they need to leave if they think we are wrong about women's role in the church."[11] This approach is lacking in at least two important ways:

1. First, the appeal to the denomination's creed, the *Statement of Beliefs,* is an appeal to human authority. Appeal to another denominational creed would likely yield another answer. This is certainly one of the reasons we have over 34,000 denominations and growing within the broad community of Christianity. It is past time that those who claim to be disciples of Jesus stop appealing to the councils of men to settle matters of faith. There is but one authority: the divinely inspired Word of God contained in the Bible.

2. Who is to determine which doctrines of Christ are more important than others? Who decides that one class of doctrines can be dismissed as cultural and another bound upon people of all ages? This is denominationalism at its very core. In the

---

11 Worldwide Church of God Doctrinal Team (preface by Joseph Tkach), *Women in Church Leadership: An Introduction* (2004), www.wcg.org/lit/church/ministry/women2.htm, Worldwide Church of God, Glendora, CA.

end, we may, in fact, decide that some Biblical teaching is culturally based and not applicable today, but this whole area is a very slippery slope. We must proceed with great caution… and lots of prayer. Surely, determination of what is based on cultural custom and is not binding today can be decided from inspired text, not the creeds or councils of men, and certainly not by men passing judgment on which doctrines have more or less importance.

So the question before us is should the prohibitions against women occupying positions of leadership in the church be dismissed as simply a cultural custom of that early time, or are they prohibitions to be honored today? Going back to the creation account in Genesis 1 and 2, we find that man was created before woman, but that of itself doesn't seem to indicate inferior position except the apostle Paul used it as part of his argument that women not teach or have authority over man. (1 Timothy 2:13) The fact is, both were made in the image of God (Genesis 1:27), indicating clearly that females are in no way inferior to males. The creation record emphasizes the complementary nature of the male and female rather than woman being in subjection to man. (Genesis, 1:18-20)

Then sin entered the picture. Satan deceived Eve. Consequently, she ate of the forbidden fruit, and then gave to her husband who also ate. (Genesis 3:2-13) Among the punishments pronounced, God said to the woman, "Your desire shall be to your husband, And he shall rule over you." (Genesis 3:16) This constituted a significant change in their relationship. Nowhere before in the divine record do we find clear indication that the man was to rule over woman. As a consequence of the first fall from grace, woman was placed in subjection to man.

In his inspired letter to Timothy, Paul enlightens further on this new relationship between men and women as a means of explaining his prohibition against women teaching or having authority over men: "Let a woman learn in silence with all submission. And I do not permit a woman to teach or have authority over a man,

Women as Preachers and Elders

but to be in silence. For Adam was formed first, then Eve. And Adam was not deceived, but the woman being deceived, fell into transgression." (1 Timothy 2:11-14) It seems clear that Paul did not view any prohibition on women occupying certain positions in the church as a cultural matter. He went back to the beginning to explain the reason for the prohibition. Clearly, it is a principle of timeless truth which transcends many generations and cultures. By what reasoning can we dismiss this matter as a cultural custom of Paul's time and allow women to have authority over men in the church today?

The Church and Culture

The church exists and functions by the supreme authority of the God of heaven. He ordained the church "before the foundation of the world, to be holy and without blame before Him in love." (Ephesians 1:3, 4) Cultures and their customs are created and modified by men. Cultural customs will necessarily have their impact upon the church because, though we are destined for a better place, we live in this world, each in the culture to which she was born or that he has chosen to embrace. The bottom line is the church is to shape and change the culture in which it lives, not the other way around.

Let us take firm hold of the principle that all we do in word or deed will be by the authority of God as we are able to glean from the Bible. Never let it be said that the church must change because the culture has changed. To be sure, when we dismiss any matter of scriptural authority on the basis of cultural custom we are on the precipice of a slippery slope for which there is no good stopping point. Prayer is an indispensable part of the process, as are sincere respect and love for God's truth.

When truth finds its definition in a person or a culture, anything can become "true." History proclaims the absurdity of such a view. There were cultures who, in their ignorance, believed that falling objects increased their speed of fall without limit, the earth is flat, and patients should be bled to get well. Facts proved them wrong. If we draw truth from anything but factual evidence, we are stuck with relativism, a system of personal "truth" and a world of no higher authority as in the days before Israel had a king when "everyone did what was right in his own eyes." (Judges 21:25)

Someone might inquire, "Why didn't God make all matters of truth clearer? Why do we have to grapple prayerfully with any part of Biblical authority and hope that we have interpreted correctly?" Maybe the Lord included such matters as a means of testing our love for Him and the truth. Maybe He wants to see how easily we dismiss such matters as trivial, or how quickly we will follow the crowd, or how readily we roll over to the pressures of culture. And when we discuss and disagree among ourselves, will we demonstrate love for the other, or will we bite and devour?

One last thought: what I have written is my current thinking on what I have called cultural matters. I hope to grow and increase in both faith and understanding. Perhaps you have seen a flaw in my reasoning or a pertinent passage I have overlooked. Please let me know your thoughts and questions that I might improve my understanding: charlie@clarionword.com.

Rules to Remember

Observe the Law of Exclusion

The law of exclusion is another important guideline. When a passage of Scripture authorizes something to be done and includes who should do it and how it should be done, no other individuals or ways of doing it are included. This may at first seem an undue restriction. Many are the times I have heard, "Oh, it doesn't make any difference to the Lord how you do it, as long as you do it," or "The Lord loves everyone and will accept all on any terms."

The law of exclusion is a principle that applies to much more than just Bible study; it governs every aspect of life. The popular CBS TV show, Who Wants to Be a Millionaire, may serve to illustrate. It is not enough for the contestants to want the million dollars. To be on the show they must first qualify by passing a test. Anyone who does not take the test or takes it and fails is excluded. Those who pass the test must then travel to New York City. Anyone who passes the test but for some reason fails to make the trip is excluded from play, barred from the opportunity to win the money. Contestants must take the hot seat when told and play the game according to rules set by the producer. Suppose a contestant decided to do cartwheels around the set to earn the money. It wouldn't work. He or she would be immediately excluded from play. And as we often see, anyone who fails to correctly answer all fifteen questions is excluded from receiving full payout.

In this example, there are several points of exclusion. Those who are included in play are only those who pass the test and travel to New York. All others are excluded. How they play is also important. Anyone who will not play by the rules is excluded. The law of exclusion says that when the qualifications are specified with the authorization to do something, anyone not qualified is not authorized to do it. Equally, the law mandates that when the manner of doing something is specified with the authorization for doing it, any other manner of doing it is excluded.

Let's see how this works in a Biblical example. Do you remember the story of Naaman, the leprous commander of the Syrian Army? (2 Kings 5:1-15) Naaman traveled far to seek a cure by God's power at the hand of Elisha, the prophet of God. Elisha sent a messenger to tell him to dip seven times in the Jordan River, and he would be cleansed. Naaman became enraged. *Surely*, he thought, *Elisha will come out to me, wave his hand over the place and call on the name of the Lord his God.* He reasoned there are much better rivers in Syria than the insignificant muddy Jordon, "Could I not wash in them and be clean?" (2 Kings 5:12) Can you see the law of exclusion at work? Elisha, by the power of God, authorized the removal of Naaman's leprosy. But the thing to be done could not be done any other way, and what was authorized to be done to Naaman was not authority for the cleansing of any other leper. Every other leper was excluded, and every other manner of cleansing was excluded.

When applying the commands of God, be careful to observe any qualifying requirements there may be as a consequence of the law of exclusion.

Ask If Generic or Specific Authority

In addition to applying the law of exclusion, another way to distinguish that which is authorized from that which is excluded is to ask if the authority is general or specific. If the Bible specifies exactly what may be done, all other equivalent matters are excluded. In this case, we have *specific authority*. On the other hand, if there are no specifics of how, when and where, the thing authorized may be done; we have *general* or *generic authority*.

To notice some examples, let's consider what authority there may be in the New Testament for music in worship. Paul instructed the Ephesians, "…speaking to one another in psalms, hymns and spiritual songs, singing and making melody in your hearts to the Lord." (Ephesians 5:19) He gave a similar instruction to the Colossians: "Let the word of Christ dwell in you richly in all wisdom, teaching and admonishing one another in psalms and hymns and spiritual songs, singing with grace in your hearts to the Lord." (Colossians 3:16) Given these, the authority for making music in worship is specific: sing. If he had said to them, "Make music," there would be general authority to choose any kind of music desired: singing, instrumental music, humming or whistling. Since he mentioned singing only, there is no authority for any other kind of music.

Having established that there is authority to sing, the question comes, "Sing what?" The inspired authority Paul gave was specific – psalms, hymns and spiritual songs. How about country, rock, ballads or folk? No songs are authorized unless they can be classified as psalms, hymns or spiritual songs. Now, take a closer look at what Paul authorized. Would any spiritual song be authorized? Sure. Paul did not specify any particular spiritual songs. So, for the universe of spiritual songs he gave general authority to sing any.

The fact that most of today's world of Christianity uses instrumental music in worship does not mean it is authorized. Actually, musical instruments in worship was added long after the first century. Secular history records that it was not a part of Christian worship for at least six hundred years, and did not become widespread for another thousand plus years.

Some have argued that they like instrumental music, or it makes the worship seem to them more spiritual, or it helps establish the correct pitch and pace for congregational singing, or it is traditional at their church, or the Bible does not condemn it. None of these constitute divine authority for using an instrument, and those who use it, do so on human authority.

Listen to Scripture's Silence

It may at first seem odd, but the silence of Scripture must be respected. The Bible is a message from the Creator to those He created. We must respect His authority in all things. A healthy way to look at His message is that in it we find the authority of God to do all that is good and right. Actually, this is a scriptural position. Remember what Paul wrote: "…whatever you do in word or deed, do all in the name of the Lord Jesus,…" (Colossians 3:17) What does it mean to do something in someone's name? If I transact business in your name, it implies that you have authorized me to conduct that business. A spokesman for the president of our country, speaking in his name, says only those things the president has authorized him to say.

When such authority is given, it is not necessary to name everything that is excluded from the authority. For example, if you give me the authority to buy for you a new fishing boat, you don't have to say, "You cannot buy for me a car, a house, a yacht, an airplane, etc., etc." Giving authority to do a thing automatically limits that authority to the things stated. Remember the law of exclusion?

Suppose a parent gave a twelve-year-old son five dollars and said, "Ride your bike to the store and buy a loaf of bread." It should not be necessary to say don't roller blade or ice skate there. Nor should the parent have to enumerate all of the things that the child should not buy with the remainder of the five dollars: candy, ice cream, potato chips, bubble gum, etc. Permission to travel another way and to buy other things is excluded in the stated authority. Silence about these other things does not authorize their inclusion.

We have no trouble recognizing and respecting these limits on authority in most areas of life, and should have no trouble with most of what the Bible authorizes. Notice this example: the Hebrews writer makes the argument that there was a change in the priesthood. He stated that Jesus was a high priest of another order, not of the Levitical priesthood: "For the priesthood being changed, of necessity there is also a change of law. For He of whom these things are spoken belongs to another tribe, from which no man has officiated at the altar. For it is evident that our Lord arose from Judah, of which tribe Moses spoke nothing concerning priesthood." (Hebrews 7:12-14) The Law of Moses provided for priests to come only from the tribe of Levi. No prohibition was stated against making priests from the tribe of Judah, the tribe from which Jesus came. Nothing needed to be said. The silence of the Scripture was understood to prohibit selection from Judah. Since God had not given any instructions about priests coming from Judah, there was no authority for that.

How much more united the broad community of Christianity would be if we all practiced and taught only what God has authorized!

A Reminder

The "mechanics" of God's authority are not difficult for us to understand if we remember that He is the Creator and we are the product of His creation. We are here at His pleasure. We are to live for His purpose. We dream and plan, move and accomplish, give and take, and embrace and enjoy as He allows. Whether we choose to submit now or will be forced to our knees later, we are His vessels, His servants, His offspring. In short, if we can remember our place, it should not be a difficult matter to heed His instructions and wait for His time.

Chapter 12 Discussion

1. Who has supreme authority?

2. Make a list of competing sources of authority.

3. Thinking of how authority flows from Jehovah God to us, number the following in order beginning at authority's source.

   Inspiration   The Holy Spirit

   God   Scripture

   Personal interpretation   Jesus Christ

   Revelation

4. Make a list of ways the Scripture authorizes.

5. Which of these is most important? Why?

6. Describe the law of exclusion.

7. Identify the type of each of the following statements. Mark with a "D" if declarative, an "I" if interrogative, "C" if a command (imperative), and "E" if exclamatory.

   a. Get your coat and leave now! _____

   b. "Arise, and be baptized and wash away your sins." (Acts 22:16) _____

   c. "What hinders me from being baptized?" (Acts 8:36) _____

   d. "Indeed, I myself thought I must do many things contrary to the name of Jesus..." (Acts 22:9) _____

   e. "Who are you Lord?" (Acts 9:5) _____

   f. "I am Jesus, whom you are persecuting." (Acts 9:5) _____

8. Describe the process of revelation including the concept of inspiration.

9. Describe necessary inference and give a scriptural example.

10. What is expediency?

11. In Acts 15, James, the apostles, and certain representatives from the church in Antioch met with the whole church in Jerusalem to decide the authority of the Lord regarding the practice of circumcision. Please read their reasoning in verses 7 through 21 and match the speakers below with the way they established authority:

Peter	Direct statement
Paul and Barnabas	Necessary inference
James	Approved example

12. Discuss what will most likely happen to children if they are not taught how to study the Bible for themselves and how to determine authority for what God wants of them, and who will teach them if their parents do not.

Preparing to Interpret Correctly

What do you mean I need to get ready to understand?

Proper seed in good soil brings forth fruit.

Correctly understanding God's message requires preparation. Among the lessons Jesus taught was the parable of the sower, a story in which a sower sowed seed on different kinds of ground and got very different results. (Luke 8:4-8) Some seed fell on the hard wayside soil, some fell among the rocks, and some among the thorns. Fortunately, some fell on good soil and brought forth an abundant crop.

Later, His disciples came to Him asking what the parable meant. He said, "The seed is the word of God," (vs. 11) and went on to explain that the seed sown on the wayside soil represents people who hear God's Word, but allow Satan to take it out of their hearts before they can believe. (vs. 12) The seeds among the rocks are those who hear and receive the Word, but the roots cannot reach any depth, and their belief soon withers and dies. (vs. 13) The seed among the thorns does take root and belief grows, but alas, it is among the thorns of the world, the cares and riches and plea-sures that choke it out before it can produce fruit. (vs. 14) The good news of the story is the good ground upon which some seed falls. This good soil depicts the fertile hearts of those who believe and obey God's Word. Faith grows and they produce much fruit to the Lord's glory. (vs. 15)

It seems clear from this parable that as we approach study of God's Word, we must do all we can to be sure our hearts are the good, fertile ground that will receive the Word and bring forth the kind of fruit God wants.

Before leaving this analogy, please make note of the fact that an immutable law of the garden is that seed produces after its own kind. If you sow the seed of the Bible combined with a creed (dare I say weed?) of men in your heart, you will become what-ever kind of "Christian" that combination is designed to make. If you sow in your heart the pure seed of God's Word and that alone, you cannot be a denominational Christian. You will be no more or less than a Christian, doing and teaching the same things New Testament Christians did and taught.

Cultivate Your Love of Truth

The need to love the truth has been emphasized before, but it bears repeating and amplifying. If we are to cultivate a love for truth, perhaps we should first make note of the reasons that some students miss the truth. There are potentially many. One is being careless or sloppy in our study. You might be careless in the reading of a novel with little negative consequence, but not so with the reading of Holy Writ. Prayer before opening God's book should help us remember whose Word it is, and that the mes-sage is from God Himself, critical to our eternal destiny. Always remember, the student who is pleasing to the Lord is the one described by the apostle Paul in his second letter to the young student, Timothy: "Be diligent to present yourself approved to God, a worker who does not need to be ashamed, rightly dividing the word of truth." (2 Timothy 2:15) Rightly dividing, or handling aright (KJV), implies careful reading and analysis. It implies understanding correctly and obeying what has been studied.

Presuppositions

Since the beginning of this book, a great deal has been said about setting aside human notions and philosophies that might impede understanding the pure Word of God. While that is not difficult to say, and even to agree with, it can be much harder to do. We all have presuppositions. Some are very strong. The natural human tendency is to construct some framework of belief, a value system, within which new information is processed, evaluated and absorbed. Many sources of information and values feed and sustain this framework: parents and friends, past teachers both secular and spiritual, the media in all of its forms, traditions, personal experience and prior personal Bible studies. Some of what shapes our value system is based upon good authority. Everyone, sinner or saint, is driven by some degree of truth. However, it is equally true that even the best of us have been tainted by that which is not true, that which is worldly, and that which is subjective.

Teachers of whatever station, qualification and godly intent should never become the standard of authority held in higher regard than Scripture. Traditions can be good in their place, but are no valid judge of truth. And no matter how comforting personal experience may be it cannot be trusted as a firm foundation for faith. The rapidly increasing popularity in the last half century or so of the "better felt than told" philosophy is alarming. Driven by the charismatic movement within Christianity, thousands who profess allegiance to the Lord have willingly allowed personal experience to supersede Scripture in shaping decisions and motivating behavior. The fact is, personal experience is very subjective, and no matter how powerfully one has experienced or how strongly one feels about the meaning of that experience, it should never be the the the last word of authority for faith and life. That place must be reserved for God's written Word.

The forces to which we are all subjected – family, teachers, traditions, the media and personal experience – shape our thinking and form our value system, a framework of presuppositions with which we seek to understand new information and which constitutes a kind of dogmatic barrier that must be penetrated to one degree or another to get a handle on the real truth. According to Robertson McQuilkin, "A dogmatic framework is built of materials provided in Scripture, and of logical deduction from the biblical data."[1] McQuilkin goes on to point out that dogmatism is now recognized as an accepted part of Biblical interpretation: "...a person frankly acknowledges not only his presuppositions but his entire system. Then on the basis of that system he seeks to understand Scripture. Today we have the New Hermeneutic, the Calvinistic hermeneutic, the dispensational hermeneutic, and many others."[2]

Dogmatism

While dogmatism has become widely accepted, it is actually not a new method of approaching Biblical interpretation. It was the accepted method of interpretation in the Middle Ages.

> "In the Middle Ages, many, even of the clergy, lived in profound ignorance of the Bible....It became an established principle that the interpretation of the Bible had to adapt itself to tradition and to the doctrine of the Church. It was considered to be the acme of wisdom to reproduce the teachings of the Fathers, and to find the teachings of the Church in the Bible....Hugo of St. Victor even said: 'Learn first what you should believe and then go to the Bible to find it there.'"[3]

1   McQuilkin, Robertson, *Understanding and Applying The Bible*, Revised Edition (1992), p. 59, Moody Press, Chicago, Illinois.
2   Ibid.
3   Ibid, citing Berkhof, Louis, *Principles of Biblical Interpretation* (1950), p. 23, Baker, Grand Rapids, Michigan.

Regardless of its past, it seems clear that a dogmatic approach will never yield truth. It also seems clear that many of the current denominational differences have their roots in dogmatism. What would it take to convince Christendom that dogmatism is not a good thing? Why, even its definition as a stubborn, even arrogant assertion of opinion[4] should convince us. Jesus longed for just the opposite. He prayed for the unity of believers as He is united with the Father, and as the apostles are united with them. (John 17) And how was this unity to be achieved? By everyone reshaping and forcing God's message into his own personal value mold? By compromising doctrinal positions? No! He prayed that they be set apart from the world to unity with Him by and in the truth. They became one because they all believed and practiced the same thing. Anyone who approaches a study of God's Word with a closed mind will probably not find the truth and cannot be united with God.

If your view of any subject is fixed and unbending, it will be nearly impossible for you to come to a correct knowledge of the truth. Paul wrote of those who had their minds made up. He spoke of them as "those who perish, because they did not receive the love of the truth, that they might be saved. And for this reason God will send them a strong delusion, that they should believe a lie, that they all may be condemned who did not believe the truth but had pleasure in unrighteousness." (2 Thessalonians 2:10-12) How frightening is that?! Their minds are so closed, so made up, that God has no hope His truth will reach them. Consequently, He sends them a strong delusion so they will believe a lie and be condemned. Keeping an open mind to God's Word is critical to the salvation of your soul!

Cultivate a Love of Truth

How then can one cultivate a love of truth? Prize it, hold it in esteem recognizing its true value as the everlasting Word of

---

4 *Merriam-Webster's Online Dictionary* (2005), dogmatism, http://www.m-w.com/dictionary/dogmatism, Merriam-Webster, Inc. Springfield, MA

God, never be careless with it, avoid dogmatic interpretations, open your mind to the possibility that your previous view may be wrong, never twist or force a passage to prove a point, forget about what is politically or religiously correct, and keep in proper perspective the opinions of parents and brotherhood teachers no matter how well known and respected. In short, force your personal set of presuppositions to its knees in submission to the Word of Almighty God.

Be Honest With Yourself

> *"Every man has his fault, and honesty is his."*
> Shakespeare, *Timon of Athens*, III, i, 30

Oh, that it could be said that honesty is one of my faults! Arguably, the hardest part of being honest is being honest with oneself. Dishonesty can be defined two ways. First, dishonesty is a course of action which would include such sinful practices as theft, false testimony, lying, etc. The second definition describes a state of mind, and from a dishonest state of mind springs what we call intellectual dishonesty. Intellectual dishonesty results from allowing convictions to get out of sync with valid evidence, a form of self-deception.

Intellectual honesty is essential in Bible study. It requires avoidance of any temptation to falsify, exaggerate or deny what the text says. Why would we do that? We shouldn't, but it may be easy when we are trying to prove what we have always believed or what our parents believed or what is taught at the church we attend. These do not constitute valid evidences for supporting our convictions. Only God's meaning is worthy of our faith.

Occasionally, I have studied with someone who was honest enough to admit having a faith that was not honest with Scripture. One woman remarked about a passage we read, "I see it, but I don't believe it!" On another occasion, I was seated with three young men around a dining room table studying baptism.

We had agreed we would look at every reference in the New Testament, sum up the totality of truth on the subject, and draw our conclusions from that. We turned to the next passage, Mark 16:16, and the man on my left (I'll call him Jim) began to read: "He who believes…(long pause)…will be saved." The man on my right looked at his Bible quizzically and said, "Wait, Jim, my Bible doesn't say that." We all joined in, "Read it again, Jim!" This time he read more quickly, "He who believes … will be saved." I leaned over and said, "Jim, it does not say that. This is the Lord Himself speaking. Read what He said!" Jim said, "No! I don't believe it!" No matter how many times one reads baptism out of the passage it is still there. It is still part of truth.

The now deceased syndicated American journalist Sydney Harris once wrote, "I am tired of hearing about men with the 'courage of their convictions.'" Nero and Caligula and Attila and Hitler had the courage of their convictions – but not one had the courage to examine his convictions, or to change them, which is the true test of character."[5] I heartily agree!

Things to Consider

Interpreting correctly is virtually guaranteed to the student who is willing to follow certain guidelines. A study of these guidelines is called "hermeneutics," a science that applies to the interpretation and understanding of all kinds of literature. In the remainder of this chapter and the next, we will consider these guidelines, which will help you reach a clearer understanding and prevent you from reading into the text a meaning the author did not intend.

Remember the Overall Context

What is the context? Context is one of the most important aspects of reading and studying the Bible. Keep asking how the piece of Scripture you are looking at fits into the whole. It is easy

5   Harris, Sydney, *Bits & Pieces*, October 1991, seen in http://www.sermonillustrations.com/a-z/c/conviction.htm.

to make Scripture teach anything you want by taking it out of context.

Consider Who is Speaking

It makes a difference who is speaking. Bible writers wrote with different styles. Mark's gospel is forceful and to the point. Matthew leaned heavily on a Jewish backdrop referring often to Old Testament prophecy. John's works are characterized by love earning him the title of the apostle of love. The point is, it helps to know who wrote what you are reading.

Further, it helps to know who is speaking in the text. Are the words you are reading the words of Jesus or those of His enemies? Is it a righteous person speaking or one who is bent on doing evil?

Consider To Whom It Was Written

Equally important to knowing the author is understanding something of the audience to whom he wrote. Knowing the writer's target audience and their immediate circumstances will help you determine the writer's meaning. It is vital to remember that nothing in the Bible was written *to* me or you, but everything was written *for* us. Yes, some things apply directly to us, but we must start with those to whom it was addressed and proceed from the text and the context to determine whether or not it applies to us today.

Some struggle with this concept. They shouldn't. No one I know believes that the command given to Noah to build the ark (Genesis 6:13f) was a command for all of us today. And no one I know applies all of the commands and promises given to Abraham (Genesis 12:1-3) to us today. Then why do so many apply to us today the promise of the Holy Spirit's direct, miraculous guidance into all truth, which Jesus made to the eleven apostles? (John

16:13) The only valid reason I know would be because the text in some way assigns it to us, but I can't find where it does that.

The fact is, the promise Jesus made on that occasion was not made to us. Actually, it was couched in language that precludes its application to us: "These things I have spoken while being with you," (John 14:25) "And you also will bear witness, because you have been with Me from the beginning," (John 15:27) and "A little while and you will not see Me;..." (John 16:16) It is imperative to know who is being addressed.

Consider the Circumstances

The wise Bible student will always keep in mind the setting of the message. What is the environment, the cultural, economic and geopolitical setting in which the writer wrote and the message was delivered? Was persecution at hand or coming? Were the people of God zealous to do His will or had they grown lethargic? You can be sure the writer was aware of their circumstances for they probably were at least part of the reason he wrote in the first place.

Consider the Writer's Purpose

Why did the author write what we have? Yes, the Holy Spirit moved him to write it (2 Peter 1:21), but what was his purpose? Understanding the text is much easier when you know the author's intentions. Was there a problem that needed solving? Paul wrote his first letter to the church at Corinth to deal with several problems he heard they were having. Later, in the second letter it is not difficult to sense the effect the first letter had on them. When the writer wrote, did those he addressed need special encouragement? Was the writer's purpose to warn or instruct? Did they need to be chided? Is the tone that of admonition or happiness with their progress. Giving attention to the writer's purpose will open up the meaning to you in a special way.

Meditate On and Pray About the Meaning

The Indian cuisine features marinating meat in special blends of herbs and spices. I understand that custom developed from the fact animals in India tend to be scrawny and consequently tough to eat unless marinated. It is well known that the toughest meat drenched in the right marinade and left for awhile will become very tender. New Biblical concepts you learn are often like tough meat – in need of marinating in the mind, or meditation. Cover the thoughts liberally with prayer and let them soak for a while. It helps clarify the meaning.

If you think this analogy a bit foolish, even useless, you may be right. However, meditating on God's Word with prayer is never either foolish or devoid of value.

Chapter 13 Discussion

1. How does the parable of the sower show the need for proper preparation before Bible study?

2. List some ways to cultivate a love of truth.

3. What does God do with those who do not receive a love of truth?

4. What does it mean to "rightly divide the word of truth?"

5. Why is it important to respect the authority of God's Word?

6. According to your understanding, what are the keys for determining the authority of Scripture?

7. How does intellectual dishonesty show itself?

8. How do meditation and prayer help your understanding?

Chapter 13 Discussion

9. Which of the following are important ingredients in a proper understanding of Biblical text?

   a. Knowing who wrote the message.

   b. Knowing why it was written.

   c. Knowing to whom the message was written.

   d. Knowing the circumstances of both the author and the audience.

   e. Believing that everything in Scripture was written for our application today.

   f. Knowing the context.

Interpreting Correctly

Meaning, meaning, who's got the meaning?

It's all about finding God's meaning.

When the lawyer of the Law of Moses asked Jesus what he should do to inherit eternal life, Jesus answered, "What is written in the law? What is your reading of it?" After the lawyer answered that you must love God completely and your neighbor as yourself, Jesus said, "You have answered rightly; do this and you will live." (Luke 10:25-28) The lawyer's answer was correct not because the law told him that was how to inherit eternal life, but rather because he correctly understood what the law did say and carefully arrived at a conclusion from that. He interpreted correctly.

In some circles of the Lord's disciples, the idea of interpreting Scripture has gotten a bad name. Perhaps it is because there is so much faulty, self-serving interpretation going around in the broad community of Christianity. The fact is, we all must interpret. Interpretation is the process of arriving at our own understanding. Done properly, we arrive at the truth. Done improperly, we arrive at truth mixed with our opinion or that of some man, which the Lord did not intend. Could this be part of the reason denominations of Christianity are growing at a rate of more than one new denomination every other day?[1]

The apostle Peter said, "…no prophecy of Scripture is of any private interpretation, for prophecy never came by the will of man, but holy men of God spoke as they were moved by the Holy Spirit." (2 Peter 1:20, 21) Peter is not saying we should not interpret. He is warning against "private" interpretations, interpretations that have as their source the will of man. His point is that no one has a right to his opinions about the meaning. The message and its meaning both belong to God. The message was given by God's Spirit to holy men who wrote it down for those early Christians and ultimately for us. Who are we to change it? Getting the meaning out of the text is referred to as "exegesis." In Bible study, the exegesis must be of the Divine text, not of the text from another source.

Let the Author Explain His Meaning

Often the writer will explain his meaning either in the immediate context or in a parallel text somewhere else. For example, consider Paul's statement to the Galatians about Abraham's two sons: "For it is written that Abraham had two sons: the one by a bondwoman, the other by a freewoman. But he who was of the bondwoman was born according to the flesh, and he of the freewoman through promise,…" (Galatians 4:22, 23) What did Paul mean? Well, let's let him explain. Going on in the next verse he says, "…which things are symbolic. For these are the two covenants: the one from Mount Sinai which gives birth to bondage, which is Hagar… but the Jerusalem above is free, which is the

---

1 Barrett, David B.; Kurian, George Thomas; and Johnson, Todd M. (Editors), *World Christian Encyclopedia: A Comparative Survey of Churches and Religions in the Modern World Volume I: The World by Countries: Religionists, Churches, Ministries* (2001), p.5, Oxford University Press, New York, New York.

mother of us all… Now we, brethren, as Isaac was, are children of promise." (Galatians 4:24-28) The context of Paul's message regarding this point continues on a few more verses ending in the thought, "So then, brethren, we are not children of the bond-woman but of the free." (Galatians 4:31) Letting Paul explain before concluding is very helpful.

In another place, Paul wrote the Ephesians about the mystery that had been divinely revealed to him, but they would be able to understand. He said, "…by revelation He made known to me the mystery (as I have briefly written already, by which, when you read, you may understand my knowledge of the mystery of Christ),…" (Ephesians 3:3, 4) He went on to identify the mystery: "…that the Gentiles should be fellow heirs, of the same body, and partakers of His promise in Christ through the gospel,…" (Ephesians 3:6)

Let's look at another, though a little different, example of letting the author explain his meaning. Many of the things Paul said to the Ephesians in their letter he said to the Colossians in theirs. The letters were actually written for different purposes, but some thoughts written in one are paralleled in the other. For example, Paul wrote to the Ephesians, "…but be filled with the Spirit, speaking to one another in psalms and hymns and spiritual songs, singing and making melody in your heart to the Lord, giving thanks always for all things to God the Father in the name of the Lord Jesus Christ." (Ephesians 5:18-20) To the Colossians he wrote, "And let the peace of God rule in your hearts, to which also you were called in one body; and be thankful. Let the word of Christ dwell in you richly in all wisdom, teaching and admonishing one another in psalms and hymns and spiritual songs, singing with grace in your hearts to the Lord." (Colossian 3:15, 16) Each letter deals with the kind of music God wants from us. In both cases, it is music from the heart of the believer. In one letter this springs forth from being filled with the Spirit who revealed God's will to men; in the other it springs from Christ's

Let the Author Explain His Meaning

Word richly dwelling within us. Since the Spirit is the One who revealed God's mind to inspired writers, these two are very similar thoughts. To the Ephesians he said we are speaking to one another when we sing. To the Colossians he explained that the purpose of that speaking is to edify one another, to teach and admonish one another. Both agree there is no place in this process for anything but psalms, hymns and spiritual songs. Songs of a secular nature, no matter how popular, would be an addition to what Paul taught. Together, these two passages along with his comment to the Corinthians that "I will sing with the spirit, and I will sing with the understanding" (1 Corinthians 14:15) sum up Paul's instructions about music in the church.

Hopefully what we have noted will illustrate the point: where possible, let the author explain his meaning. Considering all he wrote often fills out the picture for us.

Let Scripture Explain Scripture

In the same way as letting the author explain his meaning, it is wise whenever possible to let the Scripture explain its meaning. Of course, it will not always, but if we are patient and open to the message of God, it will frequently show us the way. Jesus often taught on a subject in a way the early disciples did not grasp as when He told and later explained the parable of the sower (Luke 8:4-8 and 9-18) and when he explained how the Father draws those who come to the Savior. (John 6:44, 45) Both of these are examples of where we need only consider the immediate context to get the explanation.

There are cases where a broader context is needed. On the day of Pentecost, Peter told the multitude gathered before him, "For David did not ascend into the heavens, but he says himself: 'The Lord said to my Lord, 'Sit at My right hand, Till I make Your enemies Your footstool.'" Therefore let all the house of Israel know assuredly that God has made this Jesus, whom you crucified, both

Lord and Christ." (Acts 2:34-36) Considering these words in the context of the rest of Peter's sermon in Acts 2, they certainly seem understandable. Jesus was killed, but unlike David whose body was still in the grave, the Lord rose from the dead and was seated on the throne of David at the Father's right hand. Still, Paul wrote later on this subject putting what Peter said in a much clearer light. Speaking of the second coming of our Lord, Paul said, "Then comes the end, when He delivers the kingdom to the Father, when He puts an end to all rule and all authority and power. For He must reign till He has put all enemies under His feet. The last enemy that will be destroyed is death." (1 Corinthians 15:24-26)

In Acts 2, we learn that Jesus was anointed the Lord and Christ and began ruling on David's throne shortly after His resurrection, and would reign until the Father made His enemies His footstool. (Acts 2:29-36) Then later, in 1 Corinthians 15, we learn that He is reigning and will continue to do so until all of His enemies, the last being death, are subdued. (vss. 24-28) Other passages of Scripture confirm this understanding, speaking of the kingdom of God in the present or past tense during the apostles' time. (Colossians 1:13; Hebrews 12:28; Revelation 1:6, 9)

A caution is in order. When letting Scripture explain Scripture, avoid forcing plain Scripture into the perceived meaning of a difficult text. It is a good rule to let plain Scripture determine the meaning of a more difficult passage. Have patience, dear reader, in drawing conclusions. Humble yourself before His Word and let it bring you in its way to a fuller knowledge of truth.

Important Steps to Take

Do you remember the encounter of the blind men with an elephant? The moral of the story is that your first impression is almost always not the truth. Nor is any conclusion based upon only a part of the evidence. Sum up everything on the subject before drawing a conclusion. Do you want to know the truth about water baptism? Don't ask the most learned theologian or any denomination. Don't even seek a consensus of all the denominational positions. The truth is in Scripture. Using the topic of baptism as an example, let's go through the steps of interpretation noticing various potential pitfalls along the way. Baptism is a good topic for illustration because the broad community of Christianity, from theologian to layman, has twisted or ignored it, redefined or misapplied it to suit a myriad of tastes. The result is hopeless division over what it is, what it is for, how it should be administered, and who should receive it. The first step to getting at the truth is to locate the meaning of key words.

Look for Faulty Word Meanings

One of the debating techniques of the Sophists of ancient Greece was to change the meaning of a key word to another valid meaning though not the one meant in that context. A word can have different meanings. The English word "good," for example, has many possible meanings: not bad (He is a good boy.), superior to the average (She is a good student.), valid (She used a good reason for going,), not spoiled or ruined (Our plan is still good.), worthy of respect (Don't ruin your good reputation.), attractive (The car's good looks are impressive.), suitable for a purpose (It is a good hat for winter.), competent (She is a good homemaker.), complete (It was a good workout.), reliable (It is a good bank.), … well, you get the idea. Seeing the word used in context (as shown in the sets of parentheses above), helps us understand the meaning. Clearly, it is wise practice to have the contextual meaning firmly in hand before attempting to understand the sentence. And, remember, it is the original definition of the word we are after, not the one found in a modern English dictionary.

Before continuing with our example study, we must use a Biblical lexicon to learn the original Greek meaning of the English words *baptism* and *baptize*. Vine's Dictionary of New Testament Words defines the noun *baptism* as from Greek *baptisma*, "consisting of the processes of immersion, submersion and emergence (from *baptō*, "to dip")."[2] Vine's includes other meanings of *baptisma*: "(c) of the overwhelming afflictions and judgments to which the Lord voluntarily submitted on the cross, e.g., Luke 12:50; (d) of the sufferings His followers would experience, not of a vicarious character, but in fellowship with the sufferings of their Master. Some mss. have the word in Matt. 20:22-23; it is used in Mark 10:38-39, with this meaning."[3] Then there is *baptismos*, a closely related noun, "as distinct from *baptisma* (the ordinance), is used of the 'ceremonial washing of articles,' Mark 7:4, 8, in some texts; Heb. 9:10; once in a general sense, Heb. 6:2."[4]

The verb *baptize*, according to Vine's, is from the Greek *baptizō*, "'to baptize', primarily a frequentative form of *baptō*, 'to dip', was used among the Greeks to signify the dyeing of a garment, or the drawing of water by dipping a vessel into another, etc."[5] Vine's adds: "The experience of those who were in the ark at the time of the Flood was a figure or type of the facts of spiritual death, burial, and resurrection, Christian 'baptism' being an antitype, 'a corresponding type,' a 'like figure,' 1 Pet. 3:21. Likewise the nation of Israel was figuratively baptized when made to pass through the Red Sea under the cloud, 1 Cor. 10:2. The verb is used metaphorically also in two distinct senses: firstly, of 'baptism' by the Holy Spirit, which took place on the Day of Pentecost; secondly, of the calamity which would come upon the nation of the Jews, a 'baptism' of the fire of divine judgment for rejection of the will and Word of God, Matt. 3:11; Luke 3:16."[6]

As you can readily see, just as with the English word "good" there are many possible meanings of the Greek words *baptisma* and *baptizō* depending upon the context of their use. We need not

2   Vine, W. E., *An Expository Dictionary of New Testament Words*, (1984), p. 50 *baptism*, Thomas Nelson Publishers, Nashville, Tennessee.
3   Ibid
4   Ibid
5   Ibid
6   Ibid

Look for Faulty Word Meanings

pursue all just now to illustrate the principles of interpretation. In passing, however, it must be pointed out that none of the Greek meanings support common practices today of sprinkling and pouring. They are not Biblical simply because they are not supported by the original meanings of the word.

Collect Every Scripture on the Subject

After defining the word or words involved in a study, identify and collect all of the passages that relate to the subject at hand. Find every verse that uses the words *baptism*, *baptize*, *baptizer* and any other forms of these words. You can do this with a comprehensive concordance or with Bible software. Add up everything you find. That is the sum total of everything God said on the subject.

Here a caution is in order about another linguistic trick of the Sophists known as a jump in evidence. When arguing their case they would purposely leave out some fact that would damage their position. Sadly, many politicians today employ the same intellectual slight of hand. Some Bible students may also be guilty of intentionally overlooking what they prefer not to believe. But it can happen accidentally as well. Either way, leaving out pertinent evidence, Scriptures that relate to the conclusion you are drawing, is no way to arrive at truth.

Clarify Unclear Grammar

Once again, I will mention a practice of Sophism – that of changing the meaning based upon unclear grammar. The effect of changing simply one comma can dramatically change the message.

From history, the story is told of the Russian Czar, Alexander III, signing a warrant exiling a man to imprisonment and death in Sibera. On the bottom of the warrant the czar wrote: "Pardon impossible, to be sent to Siberia." Czarina Maria Fyodorovna moved the comma one word to the left so that her husband's instructions read: "Pardon, impossible to be sent to Siberia." The man was set free.

In several editions of the King James Bible and the Confraternity Edition (Catholic Bible) commas are missing in Luke's statement: "There were also two others, malefactors, led with him to be put to death." (Luke 23:32) The erroneous renditions read: "Now there were also two other malefactors led to execution with him."[7] As far as I know, all other translations have the commas. Even if they did not, we know Jesus was not a malefactor, so this is not much of a problem to our understanding.

Still, misplaced commas can make the meaning less clear as in the King James Bible's statement about the miraculous power of Paul: "…from his body were brought unto the sick handker-chiefs or aprons, and the evil spirits went out of them."[8] Who or what was sick? The handkerchiefs and aprons? Out of what did the evil spirits go? The New King James is a better translation: "…even handkerchiefs or aprons were brought from his body to the sick, and the diseases left them and the evil spirits went out of them." (Acts 19:12)

Such problems with the little 'ole comma can be more serious. An example is the answer Jesus gave the thief on the cross next to Him: "Assuredly, I say to you, today you will be with Me in Para-dise." (Luke 23:43) Notice the meaning if the comma is moved one word to the right. "Assuredly, I say to you today, you will be with Me in Paradise." The only translation I know of that places the comma *after* "today" is The Watchtower Bible,[9] though there is some debate in other circles about which form is correct. The difference can have an impact on doctrine. The Jehovah Witness

---

7   *The Confraternity Edition of the Holy Bible*, Luke 23:32, reproduced by license of Confraternity of Christian Doctrine, Washington, D.C. in the *Comparative Bible, New Testament Edition* (1969), Royal Publishers, Inc., Nashville, Tenn.

8   *The Holy Bible, Authorized King James Version*, Acts 19:12, Collins Clear-Type Press, London, England.

9   *New World Translation of the Holy Scriptures* (2004), Online Bible – Luke 23:43, Watchtower Bible and Tract Society of Pennsylvania.

teaching that Paradise will be a 1,000 year of peace on earth yet in our future crumbles if Jesus was in Paradise that same day. So, their translation, which was conceived to support this and other doctrines of theirs, places the comma after "today."

Was the thief with Jesus in Paradise the day they died, or will it be sometime in our future? Besides Jehovah Witness Paradise doctrine, there is another reason some believe Jesus was not in Paradise that day. They understand Paradise as a reference to Heaven, and apply that understanding to the statement Jesus made to Mary after His resurrection: "Do not cling to Me, for I have not yet ascended to My Father;..." (John 20:17) They conclude that if He had not yet ascended to the Father on that resurrection morning, He could not have been in Paradise the day of His death. I have two thoughts regarding that conclusion.

First, Jesus used the phrase "Assuredly, I say to you..." (KJV has "Verily I say to you...") seventy-five times to affirm that what He was about to say was true and that it should be given special attention. This was not a common phrase in the first century, and no one else in the New Testament used it. If the comma is before "today" when He spoke to the thief, it is the seventy-sixth time He used this unique expression. If not, it seems strange that He used almost but not quite the same expression.

More importantly, could Jesus' use of "Paradise" have been referring to something other than heaven? Is concluding that He did speak of heaven a non-critical assumption? Perhaps He spoke of Hades, or Sheol, that place of waiting to which departed souls go. In his sermon on Pentecost, Peter quoted from David's psalm, "For You will not leave my soul in Sheol, Nor will You allow Your Holy One to see corruption." (Psalm 16:10; Acts 2:27) In His story of the rich man and Lazarus, Jesus pictured the souls of the two in Hades,] **the rich man in torment and Lazarus in** the bosom of Abraham. (Luke 16:19-31) Could Jesus have been saying to the thief on the cross, "Today you will be with Me in that place of peace and joy where you will see Abraham and the rich man waiting for the day of judgment.'?

Isolate Non-Critical Assumptions

When you have collected all of the Scripture bearing on a topic of study, consider each passage in its own context looking for the number of possible meanings in each. The purpose of this step is to separate all assumptions that could be made about meaning from those which are necessary to correct understanding. This can be done by asking questions. For example, consider Paul's statement to the Romans, "For whoever calls on the name of the Lord shall be saved." (Romans 10:13) What does it mean to call on His name? Let's consider some possibilities to find what best fits the case:

1. Does it mean that by calling out "Lord, Lord" one will be saved? This could not be the meaning since Jesus taught, "Not everyone who says to Me, 'Lord, Lord,' shall enter the kingdom of heaven, but he who does the will of My Father in heaven." (Matthew 7:21)

2. Does it mean, as is often taught, one calls on the Lord by praying the "sinner's prayer" asking Jesus to come into his heart, and the Lord will respond by saving him? There is not one case of conversion in the book of Acts in which a sinner was told he could be saved by asking Jesus to come into his heart. Nor is there any teaching anywhere in Scripture that supports this practice.

3. Does calling on His name mean that one must simply believe in the Lord and he or she will be saved? Consider the case of Paul. He was on his way to Damascus to persecute Christians when the Lord appeared to him. Paul's response was, "Lord, what do you want me to do?" (Acts 9:1-6) Paul immediately obeyed what the Lord told him to do at that time, and three days later (Acts 9:9, 18) we find Ananias, under direction from

the Lord, saying to Paul, "Arise and be baptized, and wash away your sins, calling on the name of the Lord."(Acts 22:16) Both Ananias and Paul understood that though Paul had been a penitent believer for three days, he was not yet saved. He was still in his sins.

4. Or, does it mean when one calls on the Lord by believing and responding in obedience to the Lord's commands he will be saved? This seems to be the necessary conclusion. That is what Paul did. He believed, but believing alone was not enough. "Even the demons believe – and tremble!" says James. (2:19) Paul not only believed on that road, Paul re-pented as indicated by the fact he turned from his mission of persecuting Christians to a life of obedience to Christ. (Acts 9:4-9) But belief and repentance were not enough. Paul was still in his sins three days later when Ananias instructed him to arise and be baptized to wash away his sins. Clearly, we *call on the name of the Lord* when we believe *and* obey His com-mands, and sins are remitted when we submit to Him in bap-tism. (See also Acts 2:38; Romans 6:4-8 and 1 Peter 3:21.)

When trying to understand a passage, consider all of the possible meanings you can devise and analyze each objectively to see how well it fits the text, its immediate context and the overall teaching of Scripture on the subject. Then draw your conclusion. If you do that prayerfully with an open mind, you will not be far from the truth. If everyone who professes to be a disciple of Jesus Christ did the same on fundamental points of faith, at least some of the barriers between denominations would collapse.

Important Rules to Consider

There are some approaches to interpreting Scripture that bear repeating or otherwise emphasizing. A few rules to consider are listed below. If you follow these rules, your understanding of God's Holy Word will be enhanced.

Avoid Dogmatism

Dogmatism is strong, even arrogant clinging to your own opinions. As a general rule, there is no place in Bible study for dogmatism. Let God's Word shape your thinking rather than you twisting and forcing it to support your presuppositions. We all have biases accumulated from many sources of education and influence and years of forming convictions, some good and some bad. To make matters worse, we are constantly subject to the biases of a misguided religious society on every hand. What to do? Keep an open mind. Consider information from other sources, but form convictions only because of solid Biblical evidence. And pray that your eyes will be open to truth.

Base No Doctrinal Conclusions on Ambiguous Text

By definition, an ambiguous passage is one which is open to two or more interpretations; it is a text whose meaning is doubtful or uncertain. It seems that some distinction should be made between a passage into which some have read things which are not stated and Scripture which is unclear after honest scrutiny. The case of the baptism of Lydia and her household is an example of the first. (Acts 16:11-15) The text says, "The Lord opened her heart to heed the things spoken by Paul. And when she and her household were baptized,..." (Acts 16:14, 15) Those who practice infant baptism will often justify their position with this passage claiming that since it speaks of the baptism of Lydia's household, it necessarily means that infants were baptized. Of course, that is neither stated in the passage nor is it necessary to a correct understanding of the text. Not all households today include infants. My own does not, and neither did many of those of the first century. To conclude that infants were baptized, one must *assume* that there were infants in the household and also that baptizing the household means baptizing every single person in the household. Neither assumption is necessary to the situation.

I wonder if such a passage is really ambiguous. If the passage is approached without presuppositions, there should be no difficulty coming to its true meaning. Still, there are ambiguous passages. For example, when the rich young ruler encountered Jesus, he said "Good Teacher (Good Master – KJV), what shall I do that I may have eternal life?" (Mark 10:17) The next verse (vs. 18) records Jesus' answer: "Why do you call Me good?" What did Jesus mean? Turning to the Greek meaning of the word offers no help. Was He suggesting He was not morally good? Or do you think He was raising a question about His competence as a teacher? Jesus went on by adding, "No one is good but One, that is, God." (Mark 10:18) In this case, adding just the next sentence of context gives a clue to the meaning. Still, is the meaning clear?

We can uncover the truth in an ambiguous text by considering other plain passages. The Hebrews writer said Jesus was tempted just like we are but without sin. (Hebrews 4:15) Jesus Himself claimed, "The Father has not left Me alone, for I always do those things that please Him." (John 8:29) Was Jesus not morally good? To affirm so would be to deny plain teaching to the contrary. Similarly, it would be a mistake to conclude He was an incompetent teacher. Study the cases of His teaching in the gospels, and you will be impressed with the excellence of His teaching skills. Would His teaching have survived the centuries and had such an impact on the world if He was not effective? Why then did Jesus raise the question about being called good? The only possible answer is in the fact that "no one is good but One, that is, God." Did you notice that Jesus did not deny being good? That's because He was pointing out to the young ruler that when he called Jesus good, He was recognizing His Divinity. Jesus is God. We know that not just from this verse, but also from other plain Scripture. (John 1:1, 14; 8:54-58 among others.)

It is a good rule of interpretation to base conclusions about the meaning of Scripture on clear rather than ambiguous passages. Sometimes, no other Scripture helps. Occasionally, after you've stripped away any unwarranted assumptions, you will be confronted with a passage of Scripture that appears to have two possible meanings, and there is no other text available to explain the meaning. We can be certain God did not make a mistake; He knew what He was doing and had a good reason for writing what He did. Still, good brethren who love the Lord and love the truth may have disagreed for decades regarding its meaning, and there seems to be no way to be sure about the correct interpretation.

One passage on which serious conservative students have taken two views is Paul's teaching on the woman speaking out in the assembly of the church. (1 Corinthians 14:34, 35) One position taken is that she is restricted from speaking during worship services, but can speak in a class. The reasoning is that the context of the passage is dealing with the whole church gathered together, (1 Corinthians 14:23) so the prohibition does not apply when the whole church is divided into classes. The other, more conservative position is that a woman should not speak in any gathering of the church, whether in whole or in part. Which position is right? What should a woman do?

Whatever she does, she cannot violate her conscience. Of that we can be certain because Paul taught it saying, "…for whatever is not from faith is sin." (Romans 14:23) If she is not convinced that it is okay to speak in a class, she should not do it even if God intended she be free to do so. If it is a violation of her conscience, for her to speak in class would be sin.

Apart from this consideration, it seems the wisest way to deal with a restrictive passage like this is to take the safe ground. That is, apply to oneself the conservative position knowing that God would surely approve the most limited position. But, realizing that the more liberal interpretation has merit, the wise disciple will allow others to speak in class without censure. God is the judge. He knows what He meant and will deal with all justly.

A wise teacher once suggested to me that perhaps the Lord put such passages in His Word to test our love for truth and for one another. When brethren bicker and part company over differences regarding such passages, it is a sad commentary on their love for both.

Base No Doctrinal Conclusions on Figurative Language

Plain literal text is easier to understand than figurative. By definition, figurative speech is couched in symbols which must be deciphered. While figures of speech may crop up in the most literal of texts, there are some types of writing that are more figurative than others. We expect poetry to be symbolic and should not be surprised to find much of prophecy presented in very figurative terms, especially that which is characterized as apocryphal. Revelation, the last half of Daniel and much of Zechariah in particular are classed as apocryphal writings, which means the authors not only spoke of future events, but the message was often wrapped in symbolism to hide the meaning from all those who did not know the code. Throughout Revelation, for example, the writer used numbers to represent concepts rather than numeric value. Christians understood this usage while Roman persecutors did not.

Having said this, it seems to this student very illogical to use an apocryphal passage or any other figurative text as the basis for understanding plain teaching in the gospels or one of the inspired letters. It seems that is putting the cart before the horse. Where there is plain teaching on the subject elsewhere, it is far better to study that first and then proceed to an understanding of figurative language with the help of conclusions more plainly reached.

Avoid Spiritualizing Everything

While the Bible is a book containing many useful spiritual principles, not everything in it is to be spiritualized. Permit me to illustrate with a story. Some years ago, I was presenting a lesson on the healing of the blind man by Jesus in Bethsaida. (Mark 8:22-26)

The blind man begged Jesus to touch him, no doubt expecting to receive his sight. Jesus led him out of town, spit on his eyes and put His hands on him, asking if he could see anything. The man said, "I see men like trees, walking." Jesus put His hands on the man's eyes again, and he looked up seeing clearly. What happened? Why didn't the man see clearly the first time Jesus touched him? Did Jesus fail on the first go? Did it take two passes to get it right? Of course, not. There must be another answer.

I suggested to the group that the earlier context helps us understand. (Mark 8:13-21) It had not been long since Jesus had fed five thousand with five loaves and two fish. (Mark 6:30-44) Next, He fed four thousand with seven loaves of bread and a few small fish (Mark 8:1-10), and He and His band of disciples journeyed on to Bethsaida. Jesus taught them on the way to beware the "leaven" of the Pharisees and the "leaven" of Herod. They didn't understand that He spoke of spiritual leaven and reasoned among themselves that He was saying it "because we have no bread." Jesus said, "Why do you reason because you have no bread? Do you not perceive nor understand? Is your heart still hardened? Having eyes do you not see? And having ears, do you not hear? And do you not remember?" (Mark 8:16-18) The disciples had witnessed the miraculous feedings, but they didn't get it. They didn't see the meaning clearly enough to know that Jesus was not concerned that they had no bread. He wanted them to guard against the influence of evil men.

Then they came to Bethsaida and the blind man. Why did Jesus give him partial sight before completely restoring his eyesight? In view of the context, it seems clear that he was demonstrating to the disciples their own condition – seeing but not seeing clearly.

On my way out of the building after presenting this lesson, a dear lady from the audience came up and said, "I have no doubt we will know why Jesus healed the man that way when we figure out what the trees represent." Well, after all these years, I still cannot come up with a meaning for the trees except that they show the

Avoid Spiritualizing Everything

man did not see men clearly. Surely, God did not put the story there for us to worry about finding a more spiritual meaning for the trees than that. It is not our task as Bible students to find a spiritual meaning in every detail. It is enough to look for the spiritual lesson being taught in the overall story or event.

Remember the Law of Exclusion

The law of exclusion was discussed back in Chapter 12. It is mentioned here as a reminder of its importance in arriving at the correct understanding. When a passage of Scripture authorizes something to be done and includes who should do it and how it should be done, no other individuals or ways of doing it are included. When applying the commands of God, be careful to observe any qualifying requirements there may be as a consequence of the law of exclusion.

Remember: Listen to Scripture's Silence

Respecting the silence of Scripture is also necessary to interpreting correctly. It was discussed completely in Chapter 12 and is mentioned here as a reminder. In no area of life do we believe we have authority because nothing is said to forbid. If I say nothing to my neighbor about using my car, no one would argue he had the right to take it because I did not tell him he could not. Biblical authority is no different. Silence is not license to act.

Does All Scripture Support Your Conclusion?

When you have decided what a passage means, spend prayerful time considering whether or not your conclusions conflict with overall teaching of the Bible. Does your view of the passage you have been studying fly in the face of plain teaching elsewhere? If it does, go slowly. Maybe it is time to question your conclusion and rethink your position. Remember, Scripture does not contradict itself. The message is truth, and truth is consistent with itself.

Chapter 14 Discussion

1. Please answer the following TRUE or FALSE.

   a. It is best not to interpret lest we make mistakes. _____

   b. Bible writers never explain their meaning. _____

   c. The sum total of all God said on a subject is the truth on that matter. _____

   d. Sometimes other Scripture, even in another Bible book, will explain your study passage. _____

   e. An ambiguous verse is a negative one. _____

   f. It is a good idea to form an opinion about the meaning before spending a lot of time studying. _____

   g. It is not possible for a Scripture to have more than one meaning. _____

   h. By finding meanings that appear nowhere else in Scripture you can extend your knowledge of truth in a beneficial way. _____

   i. Since the Bible is a book about spiritual things, it is good practice to try to spiritualize every detail. _____

2. Explain Peter's statement that "…no prophecy of Scripture is of any private interpretation." (2 Peter 1:20, 21)

3. What is dogmatism?

4. Why is it important not to look for verses to prove your long held beliefs?

5. Many today seek to spiritualize everything in Scripture. After all, it is a spiritual book teaching great spiritual lessons. Is this a good practice? Explain your position.

6. In view of the fact that God is a loving God, how much latitude does He allow in the way in which we carry out His commands?

Understanding Figurative Speech

15

What in the world does this mean?

Why is it written in riddles?

According to Wikipedia, the online encyclopedia, "Figures of speech are often used and crafted for emphasis, freshness of expression, or clarity. However, clarity may also suffer from their use."[1] The use of figurative language – speech which is not straightforward – is found in all verbal and written communication. Without figurative language, speech would be flat, sometimes obscure, and generally boring. It not only adds flavor and color to what we say, it often clarifies. Unfortunately, because it is not straightforward, it might muddy the meaning, but you can enhance your understanding of God's message by learning to recognize some of the more common figures of speech.

Such expressions as "He's a chicken" and "That car is like a tank" are figurative and as common in our speech as dirt in a garden. It is not sur-

---

1 *Figures of Speech, Wikipedia, The Free Encyclopedia*, http://en.wikipedia.org/wiki/Figure of speech, The Wikimedia Foundation Inc., St. Petersburg, Florida.

prising that we find figurative language in the Bible. While figures of speech have been classified variously, scholars have divided them into two main groups: schemes and tropes. Schemes (from the Greek *schēma*, form or shape) are figures of speech in which there is a deviation from the ordinary or expected pattern of words. Tropes (from the Greek *tropein*, to turn) change or modify the general meaning of a term.[2] Each of these two groups can be divided further. For example, in the class known as schemes there are figures involving changes in word order, omissions and repetitions. The tropes group includes figures that make reference to one thing as if it is another, wordplay and puns, substitutions, over and under statements, and semantic inversions.

Though a couple of hundred different figures of speech have been identified, we will consider only a few of those you will often encounter in Bible study. In this chapter we will discuss figures that make reference to one thing as if it is another, and in the next we will look at other types.

What is a Simile?

A simile is a comparison of two unlike things with the use of "like" or "as." You might hear someone say, "I'm as hungry *as* a bear." Or, you might say, "He burst into the room *like* a whirlwind." Bible writers often used a simile to add meaning to their message. For example, consider how Peter emphasized the incorruptibility of God's Word by comparing it to the humanity of this world: "All flesh is *as* grass, And all the glory of man *as* the flower of the grass. The grass withers, And its flower falls away, But the word of the Lord endures forever." (1 Peter 1:24, 25)

Many uses of simile can be found in the Psalms. Describing the blessings of a man who fears the Lord, the 15th Psalm says, "Your wife shall be *like* a fruitful vine In the very heart of your house, Your children *like* olive plants all around your table." (Psalm 15:3,

---

2   Ibid

4) You will find expressions similar to this in every part of the Bible. Look for them as you read.

Recognizing a Metaphor

A metaphor is rather easy to recognize. It is when the speaker or writer compares two unlike things by using one in place of the other. Have you ever said something like, "He is a tower?" You probably didn't mean he is a literal tower, but that he has the strength of a tower, or perhaps that he is very tall. I doubt anyone would misunderstand my meaning if I said, "She is a walking dictionary." We do not understand such expressions literally, and we do not try. Nor should we try to understand Biblical metaphors literally.

In the Old Testament, the Lord God came to Abraham in a vision saying, "Do not be afraid, Abram. I am your shield, your exceedingly great reward." (Genesis 15:1) Of course, the Lord Himself is neither a literal shield nor a literal reward. He used these metaphorically.

Jesus also frequently referred to Himself in a metaphorical sense: "I am the door. If anyone enters by Me, he will be saved, and will go in and out and find pasture." (John 10:9) Is Jesus a literal door? Of course not! In this same context, he went on to say, "I am the good shepherd. The good shepherd gives His life for the sheep." (John 10:11) He referred to Himself in these ways to show His relationship to His disciples. We must enter His fold, His community of disciples, to find safety. There we will find pasture, or spiritual nourishment, and there He will protect and care for us.

Sometimes, a metaphor may appear more difficult to understand. In John 6:51 and following, Jesus said of Himself, "I am the living bread which came down from heaven. If anyone eats of this bread, he will live forever; and the bread that I shall give is My flesh, which I shall give for the life of the world." (vs. 51) When the Jews first heard this saying, they made the terrible mistake of trying to understand it literally. They quarreled among themselves saying, "How can this Man give us His flesh to eat?" (vs. 52) Jesus responded by elaborating on the metaphor. "Most assuredly, I say to you, unless you eat the flesh of the Son of Man and drink His blood, you have no life in you. Whoever eats My flesh and drinks My blood has eternal life, and I will raise him up at the last day." (vss. 53 and 54) Is it important that we understand this correctly? Definitely! It has to do with our eternal destiny! Those who eat His bread and drink His blood will have eternal life. Clearly, He does not mean that all who are saved must literally eat His flesh and drink His blood. It must mean that if we are to be saved, we must imbibe His teaching, do His will. In another place Jesus affirmed that "whoever lives and believes in Me shall never die." (John 11:26) This seems to confirm our understanding that eating His flesh and drinking His blood refers to believing in Him and doing His will, in other words, imbibing Him; not a literal eating and drinking.

There is another, perhaps a more limited and literal way of understanding this metaphor found in partaking of the communion bread and fruit of the vine, which represent the body and blood of the Savior. Of course, those who imbibe His teaching will regularly eat and drink the Lord's Supper as He instructed.

It is not only first century Jews who misunderstood this teaching. Many today take a very literal view, holding to the Catholic belief that those who partake of the bread and cup when observing the Lord's Supper actually are eating His literal flesh and drinking His literal blood. They arrive at this view primarily from what Jesus said when He instituted the supper: "And as they were eating, Jesus took bread, blessed and broke it, and gave it to the disciples and said, 'Take eat, this is My body.'" (Matthew 26:26) Did He offer them a hand or arm from which to take a bite? The text goes on, "Then He took the cup, and gave thanks, and gave it to them, saying, 'Drink from it, all of you. For this is My blood of the new covenant, which is shed for many for the remission of sins.'"

(Matthew 26:27, 28) Was the cup filled with His literal blood? The apostles who sat at that table with Him did not understand it that way. They knew He was speaking metaphorically. He was there with them, His flesh and blood intact, just as was theirs. The emblems of that divine supper -- bread and wine -- *represented* His body given on the cross and His blood shed for the sins of many.

Watch for metaphors in your study of the Bible. They help us understand the message more clearly when we take them figuratively as the Lord intended.

How Useful is Allegory?

Allegory is an extended metaphor in which a story is told to illustrate an important truth about the subject. Jesus told a story based upon a metaphor involving a speck and a plank (KJV has "beam") to represent sins that need to be removed from individuals' lives. He said, "And why do you look at the speck in your brother's eye, but do not consider the plank in your own eye? Or how can you say to your brother, 'Let me remove the speck from your eye'; and look, a plank is in your own eye? Hypocrite! First remove the plank from your own eye, and then you will see clearly to remove the speck from your brother's eye." (Matthew 7:3-5) A metaphor amplified in this way is allegory.

We certainly have no trouble recognizing allegory in Biblical writings when the author labels it as allegory. The apostle Paul did this when he wrote to the Galatians. The story is about Abraham's two sons who represent two covenants. (Galatians 4:21-31) Ishmael, the son Abraham had by the bondservant Hagar, represents those under the Law of Moses. Hagar is said to be physical Jerusalem, which is in bondage. (Galatians 4:25) Isaac, Abraham's son by his wife Sarah, represents those who are free from the law, that is, those in Christ. They are called "children of promise" (Galatians 4:28) because Isaac was the son through whom the promises to Abraham came and because Sarah, his mother, is a freewoman representing the Jerusalem above, spiritual Jerusalem. Paul not only identifies this as allegory, but he explains the meaning of each part. Read Galatians 4:21-31 for a short course in recognizing and understanding allegory.

Recognizing Typology

The term typology refers to types and antitypes of which the Bible has many. Types and antitypes are a particular form of allegory in which Old Testament people and events are seen as prior figures of later New Testament people and events. One way to define typology is seeing the New Testament in the Old Testament. The thing described is the type, and the thing the type prefigures is the antitype.

The city of Jerusalem is a type of the "Jerusalem above" (Galatians 4:26) or "the holy city, New Jerusalem, coming down out of heaven from God," (Revelation 21:2) both a reference to the church, the body of saved believers. The city of Jerusalem is the type; the church is its antitype. Adam was a type of Christ in that "death reigned from Adam to Moses, even over those who had not sinned according to the transgression of Adam, who is a type (figure – KJV) of Him who was to come." (Romans 5:14) Melchizedek was also a type of Christ for a different reason. David spoke of it long before Christ came to the earth (Psalm 110:4), and the Hebrews writer connected David's prophecy to Christ, the One who "became the author of eternal salvation to all who obey Him, called by God as High Priest 'according to the order of Melchizedek,...'" (Hebrews 5:9, 10)

Denominational Christianity has a variety of explanations for baptism: what it is, who should receive it, how it should be administered, and why. Peter clears up at least part of the misunderstanding if we will but allow his presentation of type and antitype guide our thinking. Speaking of the days of Noah, he said, "...while the ark was being prepared, in which a few, that is eight souls, were saved through water. There is also an antitype which now saves us – baptism (not the removal of the filth of the flesh, but the answer of a good conscience toward God), through the resurrection of Jesus Christ,…" (1 Peter 3:20, 21) Peter's use of typology is so clear you would have to work at it to misunderstand. He even labeled the parts for us. The type in this comparison is the floodwater which saved those who believed and condemned those who didn't. The corresponding antitype today is baptism, which Peter affirms saves us just as the floodwaters saved Noah and his family. Those who refuse it or misuse it are, like all the disobedient in Noah's day, lost.

Appreciating Parables

A parable is probably best classified as an extended simile. Some would argue it is a form of allegory. However you classify it, it is a story with an underlying meaning. Bible parables are easily recognized by even beginning Bible students, and have often been defined as an earthly story with a heavenly meaning.

Jesus frequently used parables in His teaching. In fact, Matthew wrote "All these things Jesus spoke to the multitude in parables; and without a parable He did not speak to them that it might be fulfilled which was spoken by the prophet, saying, 'I will open My mouth in parables; I will utter things kept secret from the foundation of the world.'" (Matthew 13:34, 35 including a paraphrase of Psalm 78:2)

Why? Why did Jesus speak in the form of a parable so often? When His disciples asked why, He answered, "Because it has been given to you to know the mysteries of the kingdom of heaven, but to them it has not been given. For whoever has, to him more will be given, and he will have abundance; but whoever does not have, even what he has will be taken away from him. Therefore I speak to them in parables, because seeing they do not see, and hearing they do not hear, nor do they understand. And in them the prophecy of Isaiah is fulfilled, which says, 'Hearing you will hear and shall not understand, And seeing you will see and not perceive; For the hearts of this people have grown dull.'" (Matthew 13:11-15 including a quote from Isaiah 6:9, 10) If we fail to grasp the Lord's meaning from a parable, will we not be as worldly in our view as those in the first century who heard but could not understand?

Some parables are very short as are the parables in Matthew 13 of The Mustard Seed (vss. 31 and 32), The Leaven (vs. 33), The Hidden Treasure (vs. 44), and The Pearl of Great Price (vs. 45); and some are rather lengthy as The Parable of the Unforgiving Servant (Matthew 18:21-35) and The Parable of the Workers in the Vineyard (Matthew 20:1-16). Parables are wonderful vehicles for teaching spiritual lessons using familiar down-to-earth people, things and events. Look for the moral or spiritual lesson in a parable, but do not try to press every detail of the story into a spiritual lesson. Generally, a parable will teach one or two main lessons, not more.

What is Synecdoche?

Synecdoche is where only a part is stated for the whole, or the whole is put for a part. Examples are in order. When we say regarding a cattleman, "He has two hundred head," we mean he has two hundred of the whole animal, not just a couple of hundred heads laying around in the field. A part is used to refer to the whole animal. The other type of synecdoche is seen in "Her car needs repair." This usually means some part of the car – the door or transmission or air conditioner – needs repair. The whole car is put for the part that needs repair. Such expressions are part of our everyday speech, and are equally common in Bible language.

When Jesus first stated this oft quoted line, "For God so loved the world that He gave His only begotten Son, that whoever believes in Him should not perish but have everlasting life," (John

3:16) He was using synecdoche. Belief is only a part of the whole set of conditions one must meet in order to receive the benefits of God's saving grace. It takes repentance as Paul stated to the Athenians: "Truly, these times of ignorance God overlooked, but now commands all men everywhere to repent." (Acts 17:30)

Still, belief and repentance are not enough. It takes obedience. James said, "Faith without works is dead," (James 2:26) and "Even the demons believe – and tremble!" (James 2:19) There is no contradiction in what Jesus and His brother, James, said. How can I be certain? Read Hebrews 11 and notice that it was action-based faith which saved the righteous. Consider the life of every righteous character in Scripture, and you will be impressed by the fact that it was their belief that drove them to act in obedience to the commands of God. Did they earn salvation? No! In fact, they were not working their own works or the works of the old law, nor were they trying to be justified by any kind of works alone, but rather the works of faith, the works that originated with God and were commanded by Him. (Romans 3:27,28; 1 Thessalonians 1:3)

It is logical and reasonable that Jesus mentioned in John 3:16 that only believers shall not perish but have everlasting life. Belief underlies all of the other conditions of salvation. It is appropriate to refer to the group by naming the one condition that motivates the rest. Synecdoche. Look for it and don't be misled. Bible context will help you identify and properly understand both the part and the whole. Simply collect all that God said on the matter, the sum of which is the whole truth. The parts will harmoniously fit together.

What is the Value of Metonymy?

Metonymy is a figure of speech that uses something closely related to the thing actually meant. The substitution makes the analogy more vivid and meaningful. There are different types used in the Bible. For example, when the cause is put for the effect in a statement by the Lord when He told the story of the rich man and Lazarus. When the rich man asked Abraham to send someone to warn his brothers of the torment that awaited them, Abraham said to him "They have Moses and the prophets; let them hear them.'" (Luke 16:29) Clearly, Abraham was telling the rich man that his brothers had the Scriptures written by those men; they did not have the men who had been dead hundreds of years. He substituted the authors (the cause) for their writings (the effect). That is metonymy.

Another type, just the reverse of the former, states the effect in place of the cause as when Jehovah God said to Isaac's wife, Rebekah, "Two nations are in your womb, Two people shall be separated from your body;..." (Genesis 25:23) This is obviously not to be taken literally. The twins forming in her womb would become two nations to whom He referred.

In addition to those of cause and effect, there are metonymies of some subject and things that pertain to that subject. For example, when Moses explained to the people the benefit of diligently obeying God saying, "Blessed shall be your basket and your kneading bowl." (Deuteronomy 28:5) This is really a pronouncement of blessings regarding the produce in their baskets and kneading bowls rather than on those containers. Job's friend, Elihu, provides us with an example of the opposite type of metonymy. He said, "Age should speak, And multitude of years should teach wisdom." (Job 32:7) Of course, he meant the persons of age and wisdom should speak and teach. Such language helps press the message upon our minds.

How Common Is Personification?

Personification is a type of metaphor in which distinct human qualities, e.g., honesty, emotion, volition, etc., are attributed to an animal, object or idea. Anything can be personified, that is, described in human terms or made to take on the attributes of a human.

When the Lord confronted Cain after he had killed his brother, God said, "The voice of your brother's blood cries out to Me from the ground." (Genesis 4:10) Blood has no voice, but in personification that is no problem. Cain's blood is said to have cried out. In another place, the Lord spoke of "the outcry against Sodom and Gomorrah...because their sin is very grave." (Genesis 18:20) The cities had not sinned, but here they are presented as taking on the sinful behavior of their inhabitants. As Job debated with his friends, he said, "But now ask the beasts, and they will teach you; Or speak to the earth, and it will teach you; And the fish of the sea will explain to you." (Job 12:7, 8) How many personifications did Job use to make his point?

One more example: I particularly like the thought expressed in the 85th Psalm. "Mercy and truth have met together; Righteousness and peace have kissed. Truth shall spring out of the earth, And righteousness shall look down from heaven." (vss. 10 and 11) We understand that these qualities, these attributes that proceed from God, do not literally meet together and kiss, nor do they spring out of the earth and look down from heaven. These are figures of speech in which inanimate concepts and ideas are presented as if they have the ability to behave like humans.

Though not so prevalent, personification's opposite, known as anti-personification (persons represented as inanimate beings), is also found in Scripture. During the latter part of King David's reign, he had many troubles. On one occasion, the man named Shimei came out throwing stones at David and cursing him for the evil he had done. Then Abishai said to the king, "Why should this dead dog curse my lord the king? Please let me go over and take off his head!" (2 Samuel 16:9) He referred to the man who was quite alive as a "dead dog," an inanimate object, just the opposite of personification.

How Common is Personification?

Chapter 15 Discussion

1. How many metaphors can you find in this one thought: Jesus is the door of His fold, the Way to the good pasture, the Shepherd of His sheep in time of trouble. Identify them.

2. Give an example of synecdoche.

3. What is a simile?

4. How is a simile distinguished from a metaphor?

5. Define typology and explain its value to the Bible student.

6. Of the parables told by Jesus, name one of your favorites and explain its meaning.

7. Make up and write out an example of personification that you might use in normal conversation.

8. Please answer the following TRUE or FALSE.
   a. A parable is a short pithy statement that summarizes great wisdom. _____
   b. A metaphor is recognizable by the use of "like" or "as." _____
   c. A simile is a comparison of two unlike things. _____
   d. Sometimes the writer of an allegory tells you that what he is teaching is in allegorical form. _____
   e. When a figure puts the cause for the effect or the effect for the cause, we call it metonymy. _____
   f. If someone said, "We have been touched by the hand of God," it would be a form of personification. _____
   g. If someone said, "We have been touched by the hand of God," it would be a form of synecdoche. _____

More Figurative Language

Flat, uninteresting text says, "Color me figurative."

Figurative language enlivens learning.

Figurative language is an important part of God's message to mankind, so recognizing and understanding various types of figurative speech is an integral part of effective Bible study. Whenever possible God's Message should be taken literally, yet it contains a liberal sprinkling of figurative language, and the language of some books is primarily figurative. In the last chapter, we considered different types of figurative speech all of which, in one way or another, substitute one thing for another. In this chapter, we will look at other types of figurative expression that you will find during your study of the Bible.

What is Hyperbole?

Hyperbole is a deliberately exaggerated or extravagant statement for the purpose of emphasis. It may be used because of strong feelings or to create a strong impression and is not meant to be taken literally. Though we may not think of it as such, we all use hyperbole in our daily conversation. Did you ever say, "I died laughing!" or "He is as big as a house!" or "This book weighs a ton?" Not only does hyperbole enliven and enhance our speech, it flavors Biblical writings as well.

Someone says, "Wait just a minute! There is no place in truth for this kind of exaggeration." If that is your position, maybe seeing some Biblical examples will convince you. David said, "By my God I can leap over a wall" (Psalm 18:29) Really, David? Of course, God can do anything, but David didn't expect to literally jump over a wall. He spoke figuratively for effect. Then speaking of his enemies in the same psalm he said, "I beat them as fine as the dust before the wind" (vs. 42) Not really. In another place the psalmist tells one who trusts in God not to fear terror by night, nor arrows that fly by day, nor the pestilence and destruction that walk in the darkness. He said, "A thousand may fall at your side, And ten thousand at your right hand, But it will not come near you." (Psalm 91:5-7) In all of these expressions and many more Biblical passages, we feel the impact of hyperbole.

Jesus often used hyperbole in His teaching to get people's attention or to impress on them the seriousness of His point. "If your right eye causes you to sin, pluck it out and cast it from you; for it is more profitable for you that one of your members perish, than for your whole body to be cast into hell." (Matthew 5:29) Surely, this expression was designed to get their attention as it should ours. Again, we cannot take Jesus literally when He said, "…it is easier for a camel to go through the eye of a needle than for a rich person to enter the kingdom of God." (Matthew 19:24) And though Jesus said, "Let the dead bury their own dead,…" (Luke 9:60) He was not really teaching us to expect the physically dead, or spiritually dead for that matter, to tend to all of the burying.

Biblical hyperbole has caused many to stumble at its meaning. There are those who have literally hated father and mother, spouse and children and other close family members, leaving them in order to conform their lives to the Savior's statement: "If anyone comes to Me and does not hate his father and mother, wife and children, brothers and sisters, yes, and his own life also, he cannot be My disciple." (Luke 14:26) If Jesus meant for us to hate our families by putting them out of our lives, did He also mean we should hate our own lives to the point of committing suicide? No one I have heard of takes it that far, nor should they. The Lord used a figuratively exaggerated way of saying our love for these earthly relationships and even our own life are not to take precedence over love for Him.

How can we know when an expression is hyperbolic? The answer is, when it is not possible to take it literally. We can be certain that an expression is exaggerated when the literal interpretation violates common sense logic and the way we know that things work. Is it logical to expect we can remove a plank from our own eye before removing a speck from your brother's? (Matthew 7:2-5) The prospect of having a plank or beam in your eye is not only illogical, it is ridiculous. Is it reasonable to think that a camel could go through the eye of a needle? (Mark 10:25) Impossible! And though the Lord said that was easier than for a rich man to go to heaven, we know by faith and the grace of God a rich man can go to heaven. Abraham did. (Luke 16:19-31) Jesus knew that. Why then did He exaggerate? In these two cases, hyperbole was a way of emphasizing the difficulty of a rich man going to heaven and the enormity of needing to remove one's own sin over concern with a brother's sin. Hyperbole lifts literal truth into the realm of human emotion thus arousing greater attention and making a more lasting impression.

Be aware though, that what seems logical or illogical to us is not the final measure of Biblical meaning. Truth is consistent. All things must harmonize contextually.

What is Hyperbole?

The Power of Rhetorical Questions

Rhetoric is the use of language to persuade. From that comes the use of rhetorical questions. They are not for the purpose of getting a reply or in any way soliciting information. A rhetorical question is asked to produce an effect in the hearer. It is an effective way of making an assertion, a teaching mechanism rather than a means of inquiry.

Jesus was a master at teaching with questions, and often used rhetorical questions in His discourse. Do you remember the occasion of His saying, "Is it not written, 'My house shall be called a house of prayer for all nations'? But you have made it a den of thieves.'" (Mark 11:17 including quotes from Isaiah 56:7 and Jeremiah 7:11) He was not looking for an answer. The assumed answer to the question, "Is it not written,…" is "yes." When the teaching of Christ became too demanding for some, many disciples turned away, and Jesus said to the twelve, "You don't want to leave, too, do you?" (John 6.67) Another time He said to them, "The wedding guests cannot fast while the bridegroom is with them, can they?" (Mark 2.19) The assumed answer to both questions is "no."

The apostle Paul used a whole series of rhetorical questions when making a defense to the Corinthians: "Do we have no right to eat and drink? Do we have no right to take along a believing wife, as do also the other apostles, the brothers of the Lord, and Cephas? Or is it only Barnabas and I who have no right to refrain from working? Who ever goes to war at his own expense? Who plants a vineyard and does not eat of its fruit? Or who tends a flock and does not drink of the milk of the flock? Do I say these things as a mere man? Or does not the law say the same also?" (1 Corinthians 9:3-8) For all of these questions, Paul did not expect an answer. He, as well as his readers, knew that the correct answer to each, except the last, was in the negative.

Since rhetorical questions are useful teaching tools, which Biblical writers often used, we should be able to recognize them, shouldn't we?

Getting Irony Straight

Verbal irony is a figure of speech in which the expression used is the opposite of the thought in the speaker's mind, thus conveying a meaning that contradicts the literal definition. In other words, irony is when the writer (or speaker) has said what he doesn't mean and means what he has not said. While irony can be properly called a figure of speech, it does not need to be expressed in language. We might find irony in a situation which is quite the reverse of what one might have expected. Irony may even be expressed when the tone of speaking (or writing) contradicts the words. Those ironic situations and expressions which taunt and ridicule are called sarcasm.

A classic Biblical example of irony is when the Jews placed a crown of twisted thorns on the Lord's head and put a reed in His right hand crying, "Hail, King of the Jews!" (Matthew 27:29) They didn't mean one word of what they said.

After Job's friends had persisted in their position that his trials were due to his unrighteousness and had refused to heed any of his arguments of denial, Job threw back at them, "No doubt you are the people, And wisdom will die with you!" (Job 12:2)

Paul, the apostolic master of speech, also used irony as when chiding those wayward disciples in Corinth: "You are already full! You are already rich! You have reigned as kings without us – and indeed I could wish you did reign, that we also might reign with you!" (1 Corinthians 4:8)

Biblical writers often used irony to liven their messages and emphasize their points.

Recognizing Paradox

A paradox is use of apparently contradictory ideas to point out some underlying truth. It is a statement that on the surface seems to contradict itself or is opposed to common sense, but when examined more closely might really contain enough truth to reconcile the opposites it states. Paradox is actually very common in our conversation. Someone might say, "Deep down he's really very shallow." Paradoxical statements such as this are used to attract the reader's or the listener's attention and give emphasis.

The apostle Paul was familiar with this form of speech. It was used on him when the Lord said to him, "My grace is sufficient for you, for My strength is made perfect in weakness." (2 Corinthians 12:9) Realizing that the Lord's strength was made perfect in weakness caused him to respond paradoxically: "Therefore most gladly I will rather boast in my infirmities, that the power of Christ may rest upon me. Therefore I take pleasure in infirmities, in reproaches, in needs, in persecutions, in distresses, for Christ's sake. For when I am weak, then I am strong." (2 Corinthians 12:9, 10) He understood well the paradoxical principle that one's true strength lies in his own weakness in order that the Lord's strength might work in him.

Again, speaking to the Corinthian church Paul used a two-pronged paradox regarding...

1) Christ's apparent weakness in crucifixion from which He rose in the power of God and...

2) His own weakness in Christ in order to live by the power of God.

Notice what he said: "...since you seek a proof of Christ speaking in me, who is not weak toward you, but mighty in you. For though He was crucified in weakness, yet He lives by the power of God. For we also are weak in Him, but we shall live with Him by the power of God toward you." (2 Corinthians 13:3, 4)

Jesus often used paradox to teach the profound truths that form the foundation of citizenship in the kingdom. Here are some examples:

> "Therefore whoever humbles himself as this little child is the greatest in the kingdom of heaven." (Matthew 18:4)

> "And whoever exalts himself will be humbled, and he who humbles himself will be exalted." (Matthew 23:12)

> "But many who are first will be last, and the last first." (Matthew 19:30)

> "He who finds his life will lose it, and he who loses his life for My sake will find it." (Matthew 10:37)

During the course of your Biblical studies, you will encounter many examples of paradox. Look for the underlying truth, the hidden wisdom the Lord would have you know.

What or Who Is Oxymoron?

An oxymoron is a statement that combines two parts, which seem contradictory. We use it often in everyday speech. For example, the sound of silence, deafening silence, found missing, a resident alien, good grief, same difference, almost exactly, sanitary landfill, alone together, pretty ugly, and a small crowd are all oxymoronic expressions.

Oxymoron is a Greek term derived from *oxy* ("sharp") and *moros* ("dull"), which makes the word itself an oxymoron. It is a form of paradox used intentionally for rhetorical effect which provides a novel expression of some concept, such as Shakespeare's "cruel to be kind" oxymoron in the lines

> "I must be cruel, only to be kind:
> Thus bad begins and worse remains behind."[1]

---

1 Shakespeare, William, *Hamlet Act 3, Scene 4, Lines 194, 195*

The whole of Christianity itself is founded upon an oxymoron. Deity came to earth in human form. Christ was at the same time both God and man. That concept is oxymoronic.

During study you will run into examples of this type of figurative language. Jesus said, "I am the Alpha and the Omega, the First and Last." (Revelation 1:11) Jehovah God described His people, rebellious Israel, as a people who found what they did not seek: "I was sought by those who did not ask for Me; I was found by those who did not seek Me." (Isaiah 65:1) The apostle John, in his first letter, sets up what appears to be an oxymoronic concept when he says, "If we say that we have no sin, we deceive ourselves, and the truth is not in us." (1 John 1:8) Two chapters later, he makes this statement: "Whoever has been born of God does not sin, for His seed remains in him; and he cannot sin, because he has been born of God." (1 John 3:9) In the first statement, John recognizes that we all sin, even those in Christ, because he goes on in that context to explain how to be forgiven of sins committed in Christ Jesus. (1 John 1:9) When John states that those born of God cannot sin, he must be speaking of giving oneself over to the practice of sin. Why? Because in this latter context he is contrasting one who gives himself over to the practice of righteousness with the one who sins. (1 John 3:7, 8)

Probing Proverbs

The study of proverbs is called paremiology (from the Greek *paremia* meaning proverb) and can be dated back as far as Aristotle. Wolfgang Mieder, a recognized American scholar of proverbs, defined the term *proverb* as follows: "A proverb is a short, generally known sentence of the folk which contains wisdom, truth, morals, and traditional views in a metaphorical, fixed and memorizable form and which is handed down from generation to generation."[2]

---

2   Mieder, Wolfgang, *Proverbs Are Never Out of Season* (1993), p. 24, Oxford University Press Inc USA, New York, New York.

Biblical proverbs are this type of saying, though they were not handed down by word of mouth; they were written down thousands of years ago by Divine inspiration and have been preserved intact to our generation. Sam Dawson, in his book *How to Study the Bible*, defines a proverb this way, "A proverb is made up of "pro" meaning for and "verb" meaning words. A proverb is for words and is a short pithy saying; a concise saying that represents a lot of words and wisdom."[3]

Every culture has its proverbs, and it is not surprising that there is a sizable collection of them in Scripture. Biblical proverbs are a special class of proverbs - they are divinely inspired. Still, insofar as they go, Mieder's and Dawson's definitions of a proverb both fit those in the Bible. Proverbs are short statements which contain wisdom, truth, morals and traditional views which the Lord gave by inspiration to Solomon and other writers of Scripture. Here are just a few Biblical examples from the book of Proverbs:

> "Do not boast about tomorrow, For you do not know what a day may bring forth." (27:1)

> "He who walks in his uprightness fears the Lord, But he who is perverse in his ways despises Him." (14:2)

> "Whoever shuts his ears to the cry of the poor will also cry himself and not be heard." (21:13)

These principles of truth, and many others, are extremely practical. I have often recommended the book of Proverbs, beginning at chapter 11, as a place to learn about the good or bad consequences of one's behavior. Do you tend toward a lazy lifestyle or sloppy communication? Look through the Proverbs making note of every bit of wisdom regarding your practice. Whatever your behavioral problem, you will find in the Proverbs practical reasons to change.

---

3 Dawson, Samuel G., *How to Study the Bible* (2005), p. 262, Gospel Themes Press, Amarillo, Texas.

Appreciating Parallelism

Acquiring a deeper understanding of Hebrew poetry is a good way to improve Bible knowledge. The Psalms as well as Job, Proverbs, Song of Solomon and Lamentations are either totally or mostly Hebrew poetry. But that is not all of the poetry in the Bible. This unique form of communication can be found in Isaiah, Jeremiah and Ezekiel, and is sprinkled throughout the Minor Prophets. It even shows up in the New Testament.

As if translating from one language to another is not difficult enough, translating poetry is worse. There is the obvious problem of retaining word rhyming, if there is such, but that is exacerbated by the obstacles imposed by rhythm, assonance and wordplay. Poetry speaks to the emotions, relying heavily on symbolic language to do so. All of this places a heavy burden on translation.

Of course, the Creator of all things including human language understood these difficulties before men encountered them, and devised a means of retaining the beauty of Hebrew poetry through the rigors of translation into countless other languages.

Parallelism is a form of thought rhyming rather than word rhyming so common to other forms of poetry. Also, referred to as logical rhyming, parallelisms are generally in the form of repetition and involve thoughts arranged in relation to each other to improve writing style and understanding. There are various types. The lines comprising the total thought may be composed of two, three or even more lines, which may take a variety of forms:

1. The lines can complement each other by expressing similar thoughts.

2. The lines can contrast each other by stating one thing and then denying its opposite or saying that the opposite is true in other circumstances.

3. Lines following the first can clarify or in some way develop the thought expressed in the first line.

There are no hard and fast rules dictating how the lines will relate to each other or how thoughts are presented. Sometimes the form of a parallelism is elusive and difficult to categorize. And sometimes the lines of poetry will overlap a couple of defined categories. Still, while it may occasionally be fuzzy, recognizing various types of parallelism is useful. Someone might well ask why we spend time considering forms of parallelism. Must the Bible student know these to understand God's message? No, not really. But being able to recognize various forms of parallelism will increase your appreciation of Hebrew poetry, and in some cases, perhaps deepen your understanding.

Synonymous Parallelism

In synonymous parallelism, the second line repeats the thought of the first, and is usually expressed in different words for emphasis or clarity. The Psalmist David uses this form of parallelism twice as he opens the 24th Psalm.

Line 1: "The earth is the Lord's, and all its fullness.
Line 2: The world and those who dwell therein."
　　　(Repeats the first line's thought.)

Verse two has this:

Line 1: "For He has founded it upon the seas,
Line 2: And established it upon the waters."
　　　(Repeats the first thought)

Here is a beautiful example from Genesis, a book we do not normally associate with poetry. Lamech spoke to his wives saying,

Line 1: "Adah and Zillach, hear my voice;
Line 2: Wives of Lamech, listen to my speech." (Genesis 4:23)

Notice the grammatical balance, the variation in the way he addressed his wives, and his use of "speech" as a synonym for "voice."

Though perhaps not classed as Hebrew poetry, we find this form of parallelism even in the New Testament. Jesus used it when He said,

> Line 1: "If a kingdom is divided against itself, that kingdom cannot stand.
> Line 2: And if a house is divided against itself, that house cannot stand." (Mark 3:24, 25)

Of course, the richest treasure of synonymous parallelism is in the poetic books of the Old Testament. Open to any page in the Psalms and you will easily find several examples.

Antithetic Parallelism

Unlike synonymous parallelism where the first and second lines are in harmony, in antithetic parallelism the second line contrasts with the first giving strength to the thought. Consider these examples:

> Line 1: "For the Lord knows the way of the righteous,
> Line 2: But the way of the ungodly shall perish." (Psalm 1:6)
> (The righteous way is contrasted with the ungodly way.)

> Line 1: "My flesh and my heart fail;
> Line 2: But God is the strength of my heart and my portion forever." (Psalm 73:26)
> (God provides strength when flesh and spirit fail.)

> Line 1: "A wise son makes a glad father,
> Line 2: But a foolish son is the grief of his mother." (Prov. 10:1)
> (A wise son contrasted with a foolish one.)

> Line 1: "Faithful are the wounds of a friend,
> Line 2: But the kisses of an enemy are deceitful." (Prov. 27:6)
> (A friend can be trusted, but an enemy cannot.)

Antithetic Parallelism

Synthetic Parallelism

In synthetic parallelism, the thought of the second line supplements or completes the thought of the first line. Together they provide all the information needed for the reader to get the full thought.

Line 1: "The Lord is my shepherd;
Line 2: I shall not want." (Psalm 23:1)
      (The effect of His shepherding is that I shall not want.)

Line 1: "Better is a little with the fear of the Lord,
Line 2: Than great treasure with trouble." (Proverbs 15:16)
      (The second line explains what a little with fear of the Lord is better than.)

If you look back over the examples given, you will find that sometimes the first and second lines bear a definite relation to each other such as cause and effect or proposition and conclusion. Here is another example from the Psalms, which demonstrates this clearly:

Line 1: "Your word I have hidden in my heart, (Cause)
Line 2: That I might not sin against you." (Effect)
      (Psalm 119:11)

Synthetic parallelism may extend beyond two lines in what is called "staircase parallelism." Notice a couple of examples:

Line 1: "For behold, Your enemies, O Lord,
Line 2: For behold, Your enemies shall perish;
      (Adds the thought God's enemies will perish.)

Line 3: All the workers of iniquity shall be scattered."
      (Psalm 92:9)
      (Adds two thoughts: God's enemies are workers of iniquity, and they will be scattered.)

Line 1: "The floods have lifted up, O Lord,
Line 2: The floods have lifted up their voice;
Line 3: The floods lift up their waves." (Psalm 93:3)

Composite Parallelism

Composite parallelism is a form of progressive parallelism which is composed of several lines, each line providing an element of the complete or composite thought. The very first psalm begins, "Blessed is the man...

> Line 1: Who walks not in the counsel of the ungodly,
> Line 2: Nor stands in the path of sinners,
> Line 3: Nor sits in the seat of the scornful."

The one who is blessed is described first in terms of where he does not walk, then where he does not stand, and finally where he will not sit. The elements of the complete thought are reeled out line by line. In this case, there is even a progression in the meaning of the expression. One who walks in the counsel of the ungodly may soon find himself stopping and hanging out on the path that sinners trod only to finally sit down comfortably with that which is scornful and evil.

Climactic Parallelism

Another form of progressive parallelism known as climatic parallelism involves successive lines building to a climax or summary. The book of Habakkuk contains a wonderful example:

> Line 1: "Though the fig tree may not blossom,
> Line 2: Nor fruit be on the vines;
> Line 3: Though the labor of the olive may fail,
> Line 4: And the fields yield no food;
> Line 5: Though the flock may be cut off from the fold,
> Line 6: And there be no herd in the stalls –
> Line 7: Yet I will rejoice in the Lord,
> Line 8: I will joy in the God of my salvation." (3:17, 18)

Lines one through six progressively build the thought until reaching the climax or summary in lines seven and eight.

Here is another example:

> Line 1: "Give unto the Lord, O you mighty ones, (Give what?)
> Line 2: Give unto the Lord glory and strength." (Psalm 29:1)

Introverted Parallelism

Here is a different type of parallelism. The first line of an introverted parallelism is closely related in thought to the fourth, and the second line is related to the third. Among other places, this form is found in the 91st Psalm:

> Line 1: "Because he has set his love upon Me, (Comparable to line 4)
> Line 2: therefore I will deliver him;   (Comparable to line 3)
> Line 3: I will set him on high,
> Line 4: because he has known My name. (vs. 14)

Eclectic Parallelism

Sometimes Hebrew poetry mixes types of parallelism together forming interwoven eclectic combinations, that is, combinations of different types. An example may be seen in Habakkuk 1:2.

> Line 1: "O Lord, how long shall I cry,
> Line 2: And You will not hear? (The 1st and 2nd lines are synthetic.)
> Line 3: Even cry out to You, 'Violence!'
> Line 4: And You will not save."
> (The 3rd and 4th lines are synthetic.)

Additionally, the thought of lines one and two are synonymous with the thought of lines three and four. Hebrew poetry often builds on one type of parallelism to form another.

As we leave this discussion of Hebrew parallelism, may I suggest you reread two or three of your favorite psalms feeling the beauty of parallel thought, appreciating the balance and cadence of logical rhythm?

Seeing Antithesis

Antithesis is Greek for "setting opposite," and means in direct contrast or the exact opposite of something. Hell is the antithesis of Heaven; hate is the antithesis of love.

In rhetoric, antithesis is a figure of speech in which contrasting ideas are expressed by contrasting words or sentences. Usually the grammatical construction of the contrasting ideas is parallel. For example, "When there is need of silence, you speak, and when there is need of speech, you are silent." By means of a grammatically balanced compound sentence, contrasting ideas are presented.

Here is a Biblical example taken from Isaiah: "Therefore justice is far from us, Nor does righteousness overtake us; We look for light, but there is darkness! For brightness, but we walk in blackness!" (59:9)

Paul used this figure when writing of the following two contrasts between Adam and Christ: "Therefore, as through one man's offense judgment came to all men, resulting in condemnation, even so through one Man's righteous act the free gift came to all men, resulting in justification of life." (Romans 5:18) "For as in Adam all die, even so in Christ all shall be made alive." (1 Corinthians 15:22)

The apostle John used antithesis when he wrote, "This is the message which we have heard from Him and declare to you, that God is light and in Him is no darkness at all." (1 John 1:5)

Grasping the Ellipsis

An ellipsis is where a word or phrase is purposely omitted from a sentence, words that are to be understood by the reader though not expressed in the text. The true meaning may be supplied from the nature of the subject or some other word or phrase in the sentence. It is a bit odd that the word "ellipsis" comes from a Greek word meaning "leave in." It is believed the idea is that a space is left in the sentence when the missing word or phrase is taken out.

There are examples aplenty in Scripture. A couple should serve to illustrate. Notice how each of the following are grammatically incomplete and require the reader to add that which is bracketed to finish the thought.

> "May the Lord cut off all flattering lips and [may the Lord cut off] the tongue that speaks proud things." (Psalm 12:3)

> "…you are not in the flesh but in the Spirit, if indeed the Spirit of God dwells in you. Now if anyone does not have the Spirit of Christ [dwelling in him], he is not His." (Rom. 8:9)

Chapter 16 Discussion

1. What value do you see in learning about the figures of speech used in the Bible?

2. Please describe the parallel thought in this verse in Psalm 1:6: "For the Lord knows the way of the righteous, But the way of the ungodly shall perish."

3. We often use expressions like "good grief," "same difference," "almost exactly," "jumbo shrimp," and "pretty ugly." What kind of expressions are these?

4. What is a proverb?

5. Identify one or two of your favorite proverbs and explain why they are special to you.

6. Describe irony and give an example.

7. Identify something paradoxical about Christianity.

8. Please answer the following TRUE or FALSE.
   a. Hebrew poetry is rich with beautiful word rhyme. _____
   b. "Synonymous" is the word used to describe when one word or thought means the same as another. _____
   c. "Let the dead bury their own dead,..." is an example of the figure of speech called hyperbole. _____
   d. An ellipsis is formed when extra unnecessary words or clauses are left in a sentence. _____

Chapter 16 Discussion

e. A proverb is a short pithy saying that summarizes great wisdom. _____

f. This is a classic form of antithesis: "When silence is needed, you are very quiet, and when words are required, you are ready to speak." _____

g. Hell is the antithesis of heaven. _____

h. Rather than word rhyme, Hebrew parallelisms are often referred to as thought or logical rhyme. _____

i. Paul's comparison of Christ and Adam is antithetical. _____

j. Hyperbole is the name given to an understatement. _____

k. An introverted parallelism occurs when the second line states a thought which is opposite the one in the first line. _____

l. Proverbs are found only in the Bible. _____

m. In a synthetic parallelism the second line adds to or completes the thought of the first line. _____

n. An oxymoron is someone who was born with the brain of an ox. _____

Chapter 16 Discussion

How Am I doing? 1 7

Am I still on the right road?

"Are we there yet?"

If you want to stand in a good place, you must first know where you stand. We all like to be in good circumstances, but there is another perspective on where we stand. Oliver Wendell Holmes, the American poet, writer, humorist and Harvard professor said, "I find the great thing in this world is not so much where we stand, as in what direction we are moving: To reach the port of heaven, we must sail sometimes with the wind and sometimes against it, but we must sail, and not drift, nor lie at anchor."

Most of us want to improve our lot in life and are even willing to make an effort to improve, but in order to do so we must first know where we are and where we would rather be. Further, if the journey between the two is more than just a few short steps, it is necessary to know the preferred direction of travel and where you are along the way lest you go the wrong way. This is true in the physical world in which we live, and is doubly so in our spiritual relationships. There is no journey in life more crucial to our well-being than our journey to heaven. Where are you now? Where do you need to be to be in a better place, spiritually speaking? What needs to happen to get you from here to there?

Check Progress to Stay on Track

Recently while driving from Chattanooga to Cincinnati, my wife and I consulted a map to see if there was a way to skirt Knoxville to avoid rush hour traffic on I-640. Our map indicated that highway 133 offered a way to leave I-40 on the west side, wind our way through the suburbs to the north of the city, and intersect with I-75 well on the way up the Interstate toward Cincy. Feeling adventurous, we tried it. For the first four or five miles after leaving I-40, highway 133 was well marked and easy to follow. But then we missed a turn because we didn't see the sign blocked by construction. Several minutes later, discovering that we had circled back toward the city, we found ourselves on I-640 right in the worst of evening traffic. Just as a missed sign cost us valuable time in our travel, failing to recognize where you are in your study can cause you to lose time, perhaps even draw a wrong conclusion.

The TV writer and producer Barbara Hall knew the risk of going the wrong way. She said, "The path to our destination is not always a straight one. We go down the wrong road, we get lost, we turn back. Maybe it doesn't matter which road we embark on. Maybe what matters is that we embark."[1] I can agree from personal experience that the path is not always straight. Nor is it guaranteed to be easy. (Jesus said, "Enter by the narrow gate; for wide is the gate and broad is the way that leads to destruction, and there are many who go in by it. Because narrow is the gate and difficult is the way, which leads to life, and there are few who find it." – Matthew 6:13, 14) But I am not ready to agree that "it doesn't matter which road we embark on." It matters a great

---

1   Hall, Barbara, *Northern Exposure TV Series, Rosebud* episode, (November 1993).

deal in the spiritual realm. As Jesus said, the broad way leads to destruction. I am convinced the narrow road is a *nondenominational* road.

We must be careful to be on the right road. The apostle Paul warned, "But even if we, or an angel from heaven, preach any other gospel to you than what we have preached to you, let him be accursed." (Galatians 1:8) It is not good enough to be simply religious. It is not sufficient to say I believe in Jesus Christ, or even to affirm your love for God. These are admirable, but your love for the Heavenly Father must be on His terms. (1 John 5:3) Your belief in the Savior must be according to the Father's will. (Matthew 7:21-23) The gospel you believe and follow must be the one true gospel that Paul preached.

I believe what Ms. Hall was saying is that it is important to get moving, a sentiment with which I agree. Learning we are on the wrong road is the first step to correcting our direction of travel, and if appropriate correction is made, the destination is still reachable. All of this brings us back to the importance of checking our progress to see if we are on track. If so, keep on moving ahead. If not, make the correction needed, and continue with your study.

Checking Progress Motivates

In Chapter 4 we noted key factors which motivate students engaged in self-study.[2] One of these is frequent, positive feedback that the student can complete the course of study successfully. It makes sense, and what better way to reinforce your confidence than a periodic check on your progress? Imagine driving from

---

2 Lowman, J., *Mastering the Techniques of Teaching* (1984), San Francisco: Josey-Bass; Lucas, A. F., *Using Psychological Models to Understand Student Motivation.* In M. D. Svinicki (ed.), *The Changing Face of College Teaching. New Directions for Teaching and Learning, no. 42.* (1990), San Francisco: Josey-Bass, Weinhert, F. E., and Kluwe, R. H., *Metacognition, Motivation and Understanding.* Hillsdale, N. J.: Erlbaum (1987); and Bligh, D. A., *What's the Use of Learning?* (1971), Devon, England: Teaching Services Centre, University of Exeter.

Atlanta to Chicago and never knowing where you are along the way. Are you approaching Chicago or still just outside of Atlanta? Are you halfway there or is most of the journey still ahead? How frustrating! And demoralizing.

When I was a kid sitting with my brothers in the back seat of the family car on a cross-country trip, we were always impatient to get there…wherever there was. My mother and dad got tired of hearing, "Are we there yet?" To solve the problem, Dad would set intermediate destinations, mini-goals, cities which were not too far down the road. Every hour or so we could experience the thrill of success. Often during the trip, Dad would say, "We are halfway there!" or "It won't be long now!" and mean it. Each mini-trip within the whole long journey was achievable. Each success motivated us to tackle the next exciting leg. Each leg was a new adventure that we could wrap our minds around without being overwhelmed.

When you have launched yourself into a Bible study project, you can find points along the way to take a look at where you are and what you have done and savor the joy of getting that far. In doing so, you will find reason to move ahead toward completion.

Journalism professor Lloyd Dobyns wrote, "The only lifelong, reliable motivations are those that come from within, and one of the strongest of those is the joy and pride that grow from knowing that you've just done something as well as you can do it."[3] The way we tap the joy and pride of accomplishment of which Dobyns speaks is by checking progress along the way. It is important to be sure we are on the right track, but doing so ought to also motivate us onward and upward until our final goal is reached.

One last quote – this one from the celebrated leader of Great Britain during World War II: "Every day you may make progress. Every step may be fruitful. Yet there will stretch out before

3   Dobyns, Lloyd, *Thinking About Quality: Progress, Wisdom, and the Deming Philosophy* (1994), Random House, Inc., New York, New York.

Checking Progress Motivates

you an ever-lengthening, ever-ascending, ever-improving path. You know you will never get to the end of the journey. But this, so far from discouraging, only adds to the joy and glory of the climb." (Sir Winston Churchill). Of course, Churchill spoke of one's journey through this life, but this is equally true of your spiritual journey in the Lord Jesus. For the Christian there is really no difference. This life is a spiritual journey in Christ ever and ever closer to home with Him. That journey is imminently more worthwhile than any other.

Reviewing is a Learning Tool

There is an added benefit to occasionally stopping to check progress. Not only do you learn where you are, but checking serves as a review of what you have been studying. Reviewing is a vital part of learning.

One way to maximize the value of review is to do it aloud. Have a conversation with yourself or a friend about what you started out to achieve, restate your goals and ask whether or not you have arrived at the destination you set out to reach. Ask if you need to make any corrections in the direction of your study before going on. Are you digging deeply enough? Have you let yourself get sidetracked from your original purpose? And most importantly, rehearse what you have learned.

Such review will help you identify the true value of what you have learned, and sharpen your focus on where you are headed. It will help you firmly establish in your mind what is important of the new knowledge you have acquired.

Counting the Joy of Your Successes

It has been my experience that members of the Lord's church often start out in some study endeavor, but for one reason or another fail to finish. Usually, the reason given is that other obligations crowd study from the schedule. There is an old adage that we can find time for the things we want to do. Anyone really motivated to study God's Word will find a way to fit study time into their schedule. I believe the problem is more about motivation than it is about finding time in the schedule.

Someone wisely said it is important to start right but imperative to end well. This being true, any project worth starting is a project worth finishing. So, how can we assure that we finish what we start? Of the ways already discussed, I believe there are two primary keys to staying motivated long enough to succeed.

First, break the project into smaller manageable tasks. Let me suggest that any project worth doing is a project worth structuring into challenging but achievable tasks, components of the whole project. Writing this book has been a sizable project taking enormous amounts of time from my schedule. Looking back, I can say it would have been easy to give up along the way. At times, the price might have seemed too high to continue paying. But I have tried not to view the whole project at one time. Rather, the first component of the whole was to lay out the chapter structure and outline topics to be covered in each chapter. Next, I worked on each chapter in turn as a project in itself. While envisioning completion of the whole project might at times have seemed insurmountable, writing just one chapter has not been too daunting a task to complete. Though I have not yet completed the whole project, I can see the end. I doubt I would have gotten this far without first defining smaller mini-projects, manageable tasks with their own achievable goals.

The second key is focusing on the joy of study. I have tried to convince you from almost the first page that there is joy in study. I truly believe there is, mainly because I have known such joy. I have found it in studying computer technology and in history. I have even found joy in studying things I did not at first find interesting. Interest developed as part of the process. This is because of the principle Jesus stated when He said, "…where your treasure is, there will your heart be also." (Matthew 6:21) Put your time, energies and other resources (your treasures) into study of some subject and your interest (your heart) will develop in that direction. My point is, you can find joy in studying most anything, especially matters that interest you or satisfy a personal need.

If this principle is true regarding the study of worldly matters, surely it is true regarding study of God's will. If we can find joy in discovering new things in our physical surrounding, how much more joy there is awaiting the diligent student of the Bible. There is the joy of discovery that awaits any student delving into new concepts and ideas, new characters and places. But beyond that there is the indescribable joy of the believer who, as a result of the faith developed by his or her study, becomes a disciple of the Lord Jesus Christ and goes on to strengthen the hope that there is an eternal home waiting for her or him.

All down through history humankind has searched in many places and ways for joy. Some of those reading these words, especially of the young, will spend years pursuing some earthly goal in search of happiness or wealth, or perhaps fame. The wise will learn from the experience of others who have gone down that road and not found that for which they were looking. There is no joy in –

Unbelief – Voltaire, an infidel, wrote: "I wish I had never been born."

Pleasure – Lord Byron lived a life of pleasure, and then wrote: "The worm, the canker, and grief are mine alone."

Money -- Jay Gould, the American millionaire, had plenty of money, but no joy. When dying, he said: "I suppose I am the most miserable man on earth."

Position and Fame – Lord Beaconsfield who accumulated both power and fame, wrote: "Youth is a mistake; manhood a struggle; old age a regret."

Counting the Joy of Your Successes

Military Glory – After Alexander the Great had conquered the known world in his time, he sat in his tent weeping and said, "There are no more worlds to conquer."

The joy you derive from studying God's Word and obediently following His Son will not disappoint, nor will it be taken away. The sincere and diligent Bible student has everything to gain, and nothing to lose. Define for yourself a worthwhile Biblical subject to study, break it up into achievable tasks and go to it, motivating yourself along the road until you have reached your goal. As you learn, live it and teach it. You will be pleased, and so will your Father in Heaven. And you will be one step closer to an eternal home with Him.

Chapter 17 Discussion

1. What are the dangers of not knowing where you are in your faith?   Can you think of relative Scriptures?

2. What could result from aimlessly studying the Bible without a plan or thought out direction?

3. If you are engaged in a lengthy study project, at what points should you stop to review what you have learned and check on your progress?

4. When you do stop to review, what questions would it be useful to ask?

5. Do you see any advantage in reviewing with a friend what you have learned? If so, what is it? If not, why not?

6. List the things that give you the most joy. Be honest.

7. Now consider your list. Are you satisfied with the number of spiritual things on the list? What should be added?

8. Is Bible study one of those listed? If not, why not?

9. How can you increase your interest and joy in studying God's Word?

Chapter 17 Discussion

Index of Subjects

Index of Subjects

Pharisees 148, 209
Piano Concerto No. 21, Mozart's 134
Planning
  the importance of 124
  to review 128
Plenary inspiration 153
Poetry, Hebrew
  antithetic parallelism 238
  climactic parallelism 240
  composite parallelism 240
  eclectic parallelism 241
  introverted parallelism 241
  parallelism 236
  rhyming 236
  staircase parallelism 239–240
  study of 32
  synonymous parallelism 237
  synthetic parallelism 239
Polycarp 11
Pope John Paul II 145
Prayer 109
Prayer, the value of 109
Praying 109
Premillennialism 70
Presuppositions 183
Project
  scoping yours 122
Prophecy 31–32, 99
  mathematical odds 32–33
Proverb 234
Pure research 79
Purity
  Bible claims 4
  every word of God 4
Purpose, defining your 122

Q

Questions
  about Bible characters 126
  about passages and books 125
  about topics 126
  about word meanings 125

asking 3 important 105
asking pertinent 125
rhetorical 230
What does it mean? 106
What does it say? 106
What should I do? 106
when drawing conclusions 126

R

Reading aloud 103
Reasons to stick with it 127
Reasons to study the Bible
  to change behavior 22
  to increase faith 20
  to know the joy of discovery 21
  to know the truth 20
  to live forever 24
  to please God 21
  to teach others 23
Rehearsing aloud 103
Reliability of Bible 7–11
  bibliographical test 8
  external test 10
  internal test 9
Research 79
  applied 79
  basic, pure or fundamental 79
  pure or fundamental 79
  tools 82
Restrictive examples 160
Resurrection
  mathematical odds 31
  propecies of 31
Revelation
  general 150
  latter day 146
  special 150, 151
Review 117, 251
Rhetorical questions 230
Romans outline 98–100
Rose, Steven 113
Russian Czar Alexander III 200